ABANDONED EASTERN KANSAS

SKELETONS OF THE SUNFLOWER STATE

REGINA DANIEL

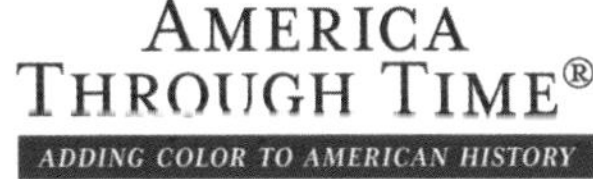

Christopher, thank you for going to Picher.

America Through Time is an imprint of Fonthill Media LLC
www.through-time.com
office@through-time.com

Published by Arcadia Publishing by arrangement with Fonthill Media LLC
For all general information, please contact Arcadia Publishing:
Telephone: 843-853-2070
Fax: 843-853-0044
E-mail: sales@arcadiapublishing.com
For customer service and orders:
Toll-Free 1-888-313-2665

www.arcadiapublishing.com

First published 2021

ISBN 978-1-63499-366-1

Typeset in Trade Gothic 10pt on 15pt
Printed and bound in England

CONTENTS

INTRODUCTION

Kansas, also known as the Sunflower State, is the center of America's heartland. Yet outside its largest cities is a vast countryside littered with ghost towns and countless abandoned structures along the way. Covering hundreds of miles from Kansas City to the Colorado state line, this book will be covering places throughout the eastern portion of Kansas. Farm after farm and back road after back road, the plains of Kansas start to feel a world away from the far reaches of the big city's urban sprawl and far from the noisy symphony of the city—no traffic, no people, and no noise pollution, just being in the openness and quiet of nowhere and taking in what remains of the past.

Down another dirt road, more places appear on the horizon to the next ghost town. There is no shortage of these abandoned places throughout Kansas. It became a game of pick and choose of which places to stop at because there is such an abundance of the abandoned down every road that was taken. Today, all of these locations can be easily seen as just a decrepit building on the side of the road, but each one, whether it stands alone in the middle of nowhere or if it is part of a small town, has its own little story of how it was, at one time, a vital part of the surrounding rural community.

All of these stories have historical roots that go through a number of centuries from the 1500s, when Spanish conquistadors explored the land that would later be known as Kansas, to becoming a free state against slavery in the 1800s, to the small town economic struggles of the 1900s. Time differentiates these stories and places, but they all started with the same hope, potential, and vision of success.

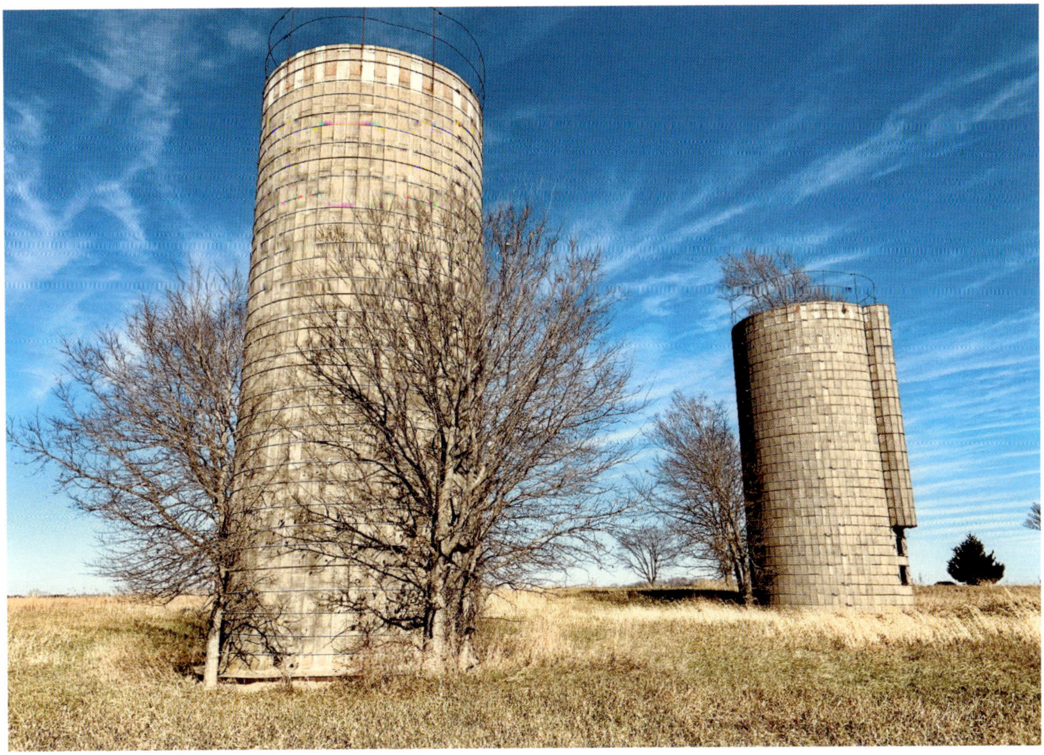

Trees are now growing out of these abandoned silos in Wellsville, November 2020.

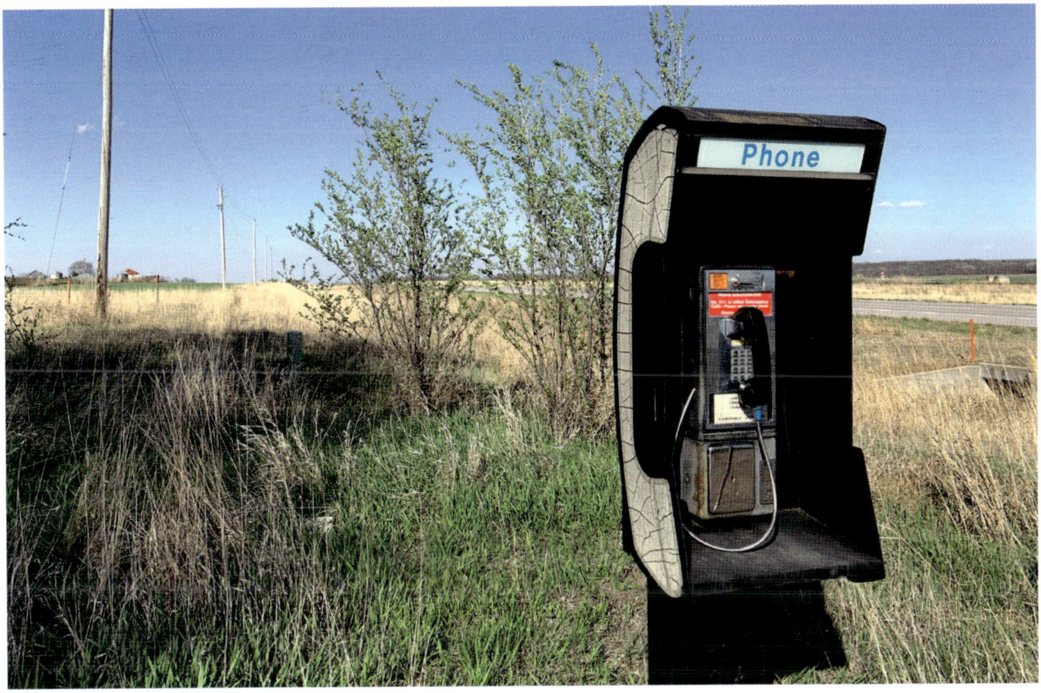

This payphone, which still had a dial tone, is located just a couple of miles outside the ghost town of Elmdale, April 2020.

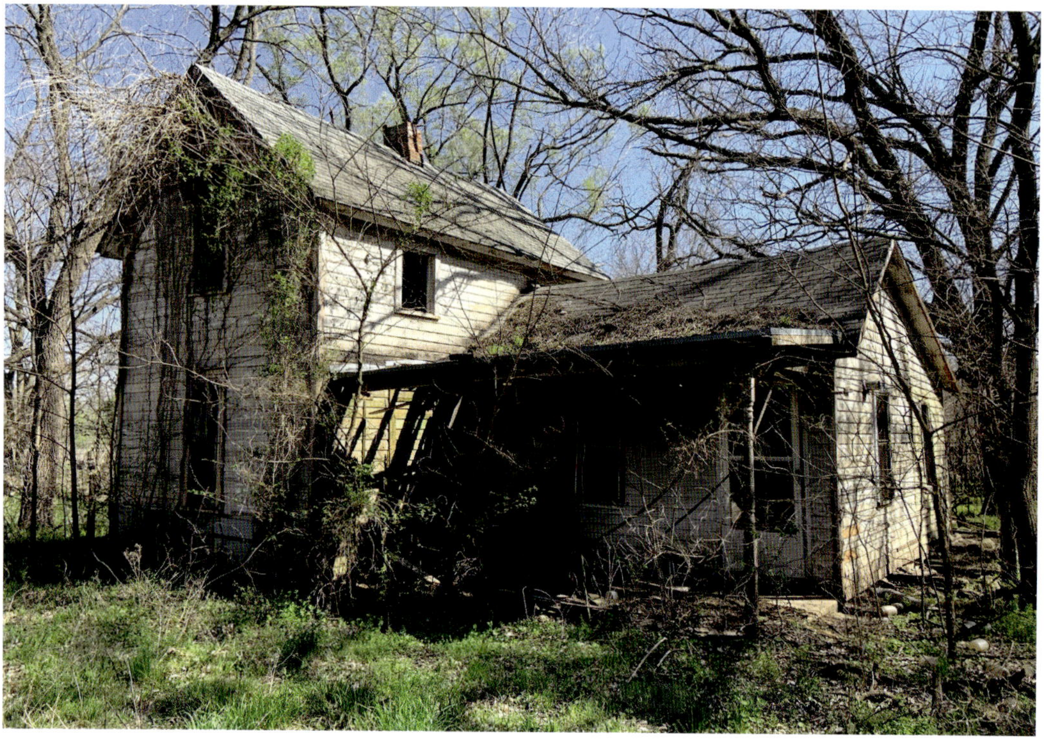

An abandoned house, located 1 mile outside Florence, is covered in vines and slowly falling apart, April 2020.

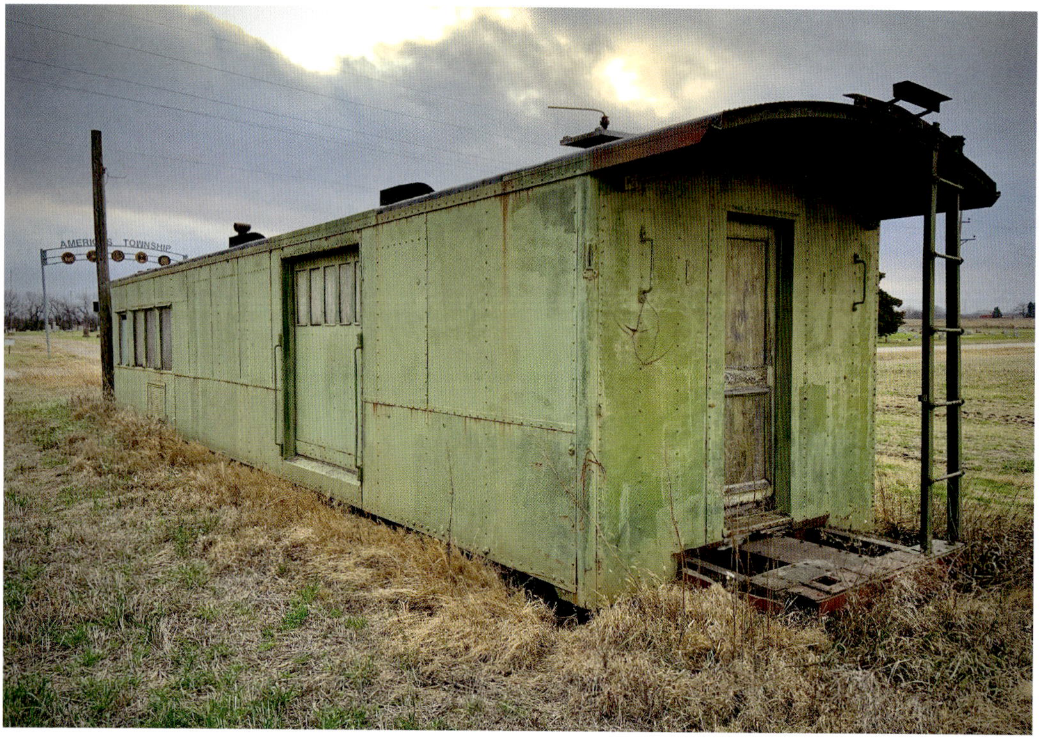

Abandoned train car in a field, located across from the Americus Cemetery, November 2020.

1

DUNLAP AND THE DUNLAP COLORED CEMETERY

DUNLAP POPULATION: 28 (2019)

When I put this town on my list, I thought it was going to be like the rest of these places—another small, sleepy, and forgotten town that is easily passed on the way to a bigger city. I seriously underestimated the history of this town. Not only does what is left of this town have an extensive history, but it also has an emotionally moving colored cemetery to accompany this foundational story in African American history.

Dunlap was founded in 1869, but it would take another five years before the town really started to grow by establishing a post office in 1874 and the town's first store later the same year. Since Kansas was known as a free state, it was in 1878 that former slave Benjamin "Pap" Singleton settled and created the Singleton Dunlap Farm Colony. Pap assisted in helping hundreds of freed slaves, known as "Exodusters," set up homes and make a better way than the lives they escaped from. Although they were free, the white residents still segregated everything. This discrimination would lead to the establishment of Dunlap's first black school, church, and cemetery in 1880. Moving into the twentieth century, the town would see some growth and integration, but flooding, families moving away for larger cities, and the Missouri, Kansas, and Texas Railway (KATY) no longer going through town would lead to the decline of Dunlap into the ghost town that it is today.

Driving through town today, there is not much of a town left. Vacant lots where houses and other buildings used to sit just add to the ghost town feel of Dunlap. It appeared that more houses were abandoned than lived in. Going through a couple of the abandoned houses was odd. Here they were decaying from abandonment, with personal possessions that could not fit into their moving vehicless left behind.

Throughout the houses, old furniture, food left in the kitchen cabinets, and family photos and mementos are scattered about, like those families had intentions of coming back for the last of what was left but never did. The town does have a small handful of residents remaining. I can only speculate that this small handful of people continue to live in what is now a ghost town for the same reason many choose to live isolated lives—either the quiet and privacy that comes from the solitude, the simplicity of country living, or it is just the only way of life that they know.

The history of Dunlap does not stop once you leave town. Around 1.5 miles outside of town and half a mile from the Dunlap Cemetery is the Dunlap Colored Cemetery. Started in 1880, a couple of years after Pap moved to Dunlap and started the farm colony, the colored cemetery, which was also known as the Exoduster Cemetery, was established. The burial timespan of the cemetery would date over 100 years, with the first Exoduster being buried in 1880 and the last two burials being London Harness in 1993 and Jackie Lee Davis in 2011.

Reading London's memorial not only brought me to tears, but I have to write exactly what it says because I do not want to change a word of his history or take away from his significance:

> For 86 years of his life, London Harness lived on the same plot of land he grew up on, the land his grandparents purchased during the Great Exodus of 1879. Dunlap, a place that hundreds of black settlers once called home, lost its last black resident on April 27, 1993.

London sounded like an amazing man with a lifetime of historical stories. With great courage, his family fled for their lives so that London and his three siblings could be born into a community that would flourish into helping hundreds of others start new and free lives. Although I never got the honor of meeting London and hearing his story from him firsthand, I feel like a piece of history died the day he passed away. London rests alongside his parents, siblings, and wife.

Nearly twenty years would pass without a burial at the colored cemetery, until 2011, when Jackie Lee Davis would have his ashes scattered over his father's grave. Like London, Jackie was also a descendent of slaves that made their way to freedom on Pap's farm colony. He grew up on his family's farm in Dunlap before making a career in the military. Jackie returned to Dunlap in 2011 to build a 15-foot-tall monument in remembrance of his grandparents and the other Exodusters that settled in the area. Unfortunately, Jackie passed away just four months after the monument was completed. Although London and Jackie are no longer with us, their monument and cemetery will stand as a testament to their accomplished achievements in the face of adversity and a history of discrimination.

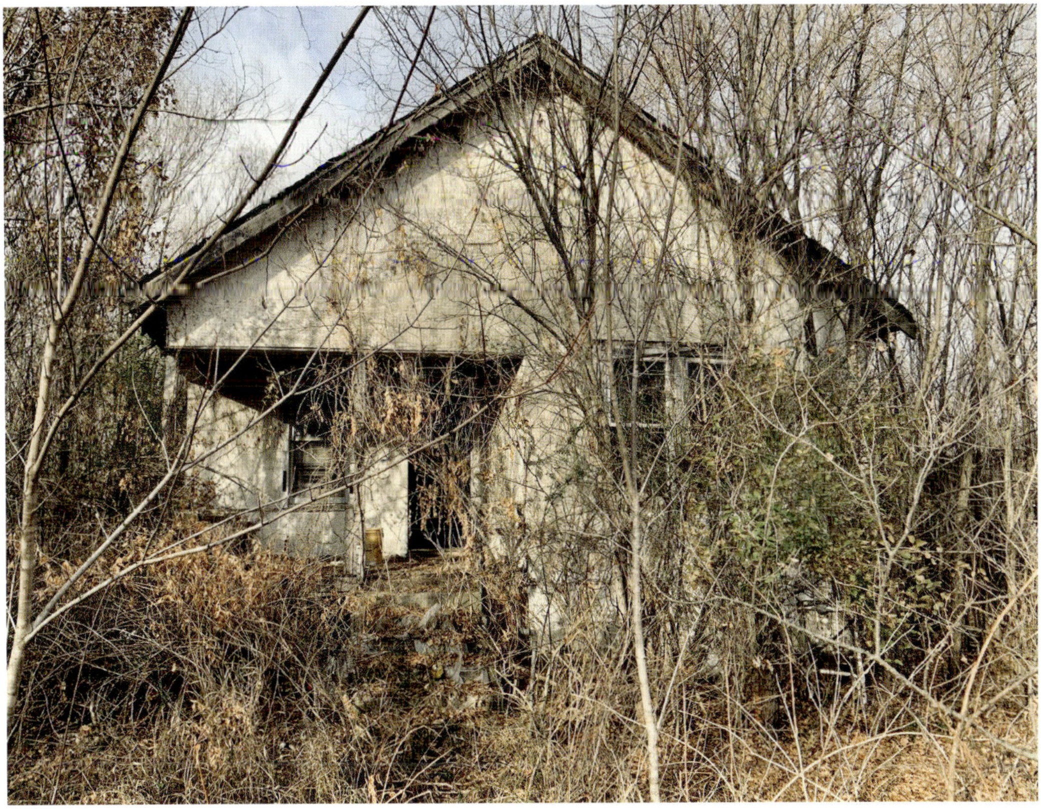

Above: One of the abandoned houses in Dunlap, November 2020. I was able to locate the owner, who stated that they moved away in 2008 for better job opportunities and to be closer to family.

Right: Some kitchen items were left behind in this abandoned house in Dunlap, November 2020.

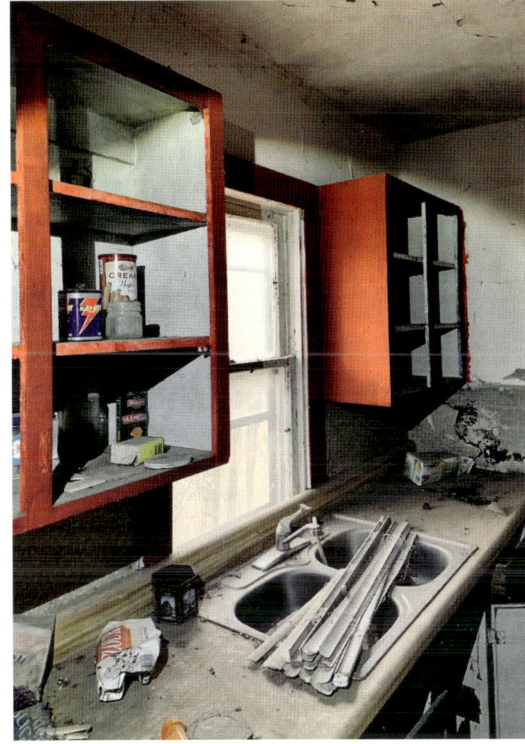

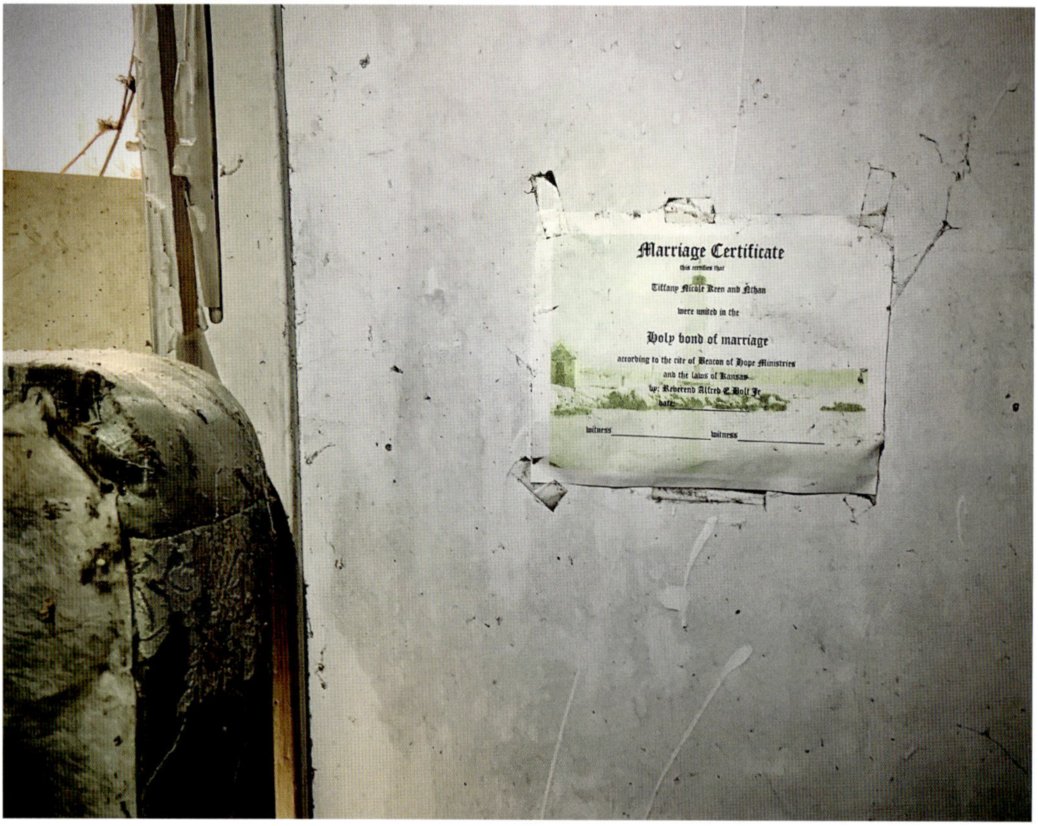

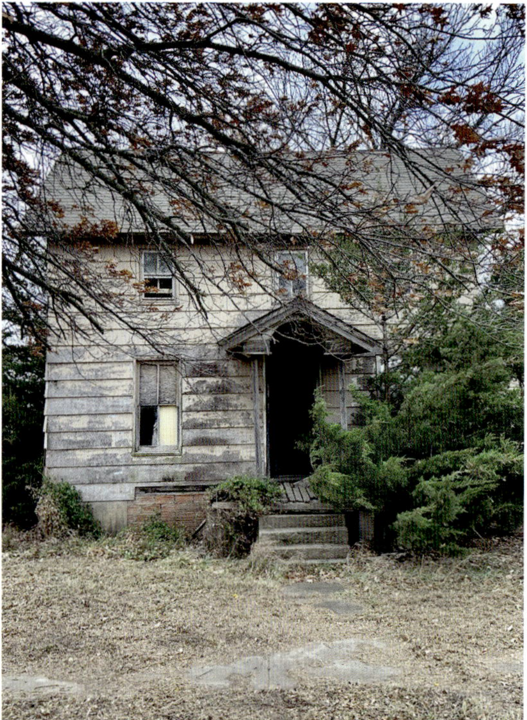

Above: The homeowner's marriage license left taped to the wall, November 2020. It has been there since 2008. Names have been edited out to protect their identities.

Left: Another abandoned house in Dunlap, November 2020.

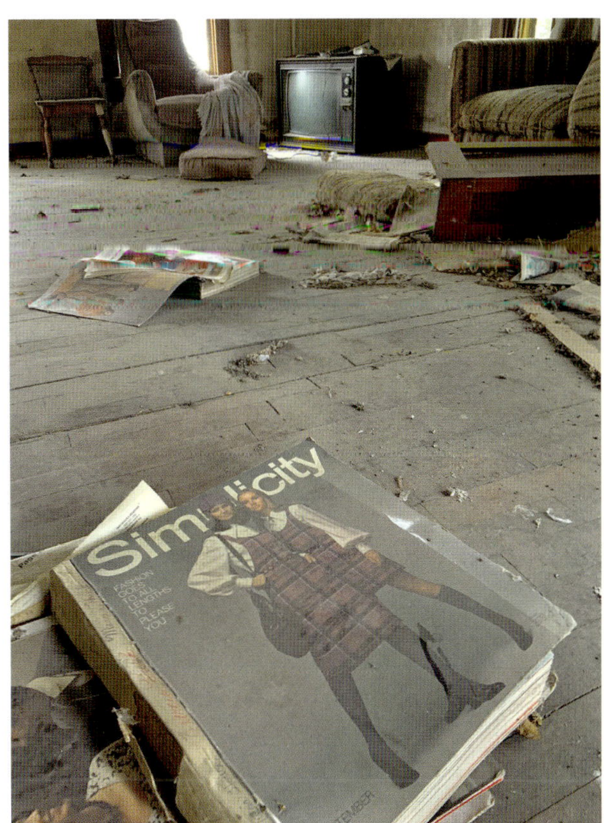

Right: Catalogs, furniture, and a TV left behind in this abandoned house in Dunlap, November 2020.

Below: Major appliances left behind in this abandoned house in Dunlap, November 2020.

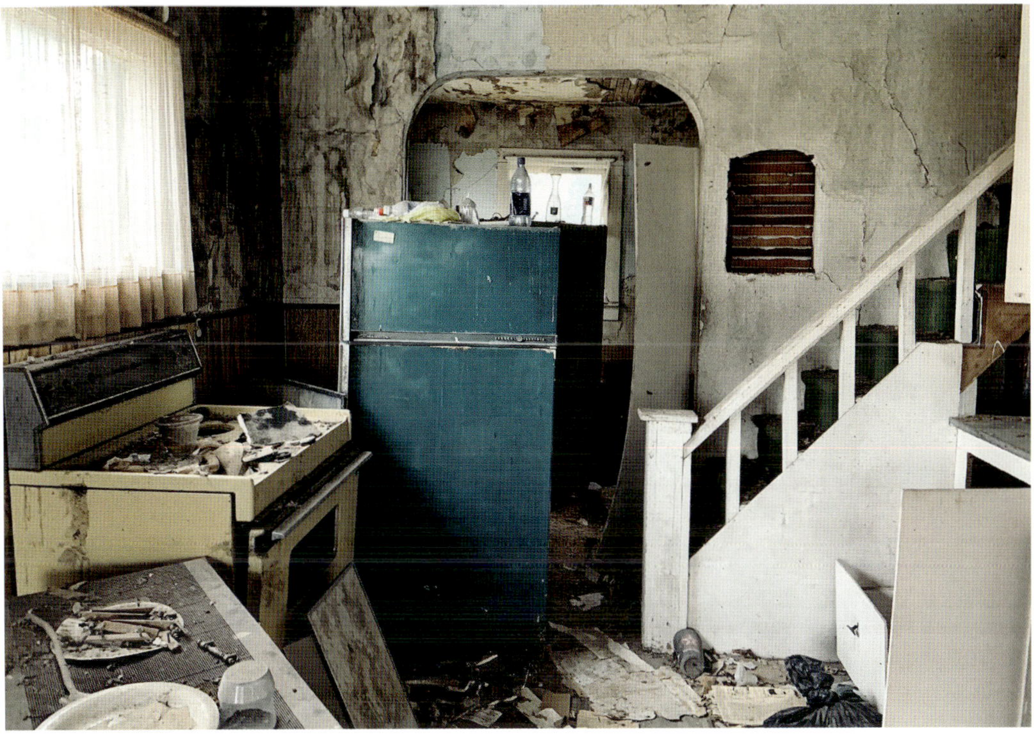

Before arriving at the Dunlap Colored Cemetery, my drive through Kansas was everything I planned and thought that it would be—abandoned houses, schoolhouses, another road taken, and another Midwestern ruin sits rusting a little more than the day before—but that all changed when I got to the cemetery. The colored cemetery told a story like many cemeteries—stories of long family traditions, years of separated love, and remembering the nameless—but unlike any other cemetery I have been to, this one had powerful emotions in the details. As a writer, it is my job to find the words to describe the places that write about, but here, all I could do was cry. I cried because there were so many unmarked graves. I cried because it was years before some of the unmarked graves got an undistinguishable cross made of PCV piping. I cried for those that escaped slavery for a life of freedom but still could not get the respect of getting a proper headstone. Yet I mainly cried because here they were, over 100 people that are important to black and American history but still separated from the town and area they helped established. Even in death, they were treated as second-class citizens. Today, the black church and school in Dunlap are no longer standing, and this cemetery and monument is the only reminder of this town's segregated past.

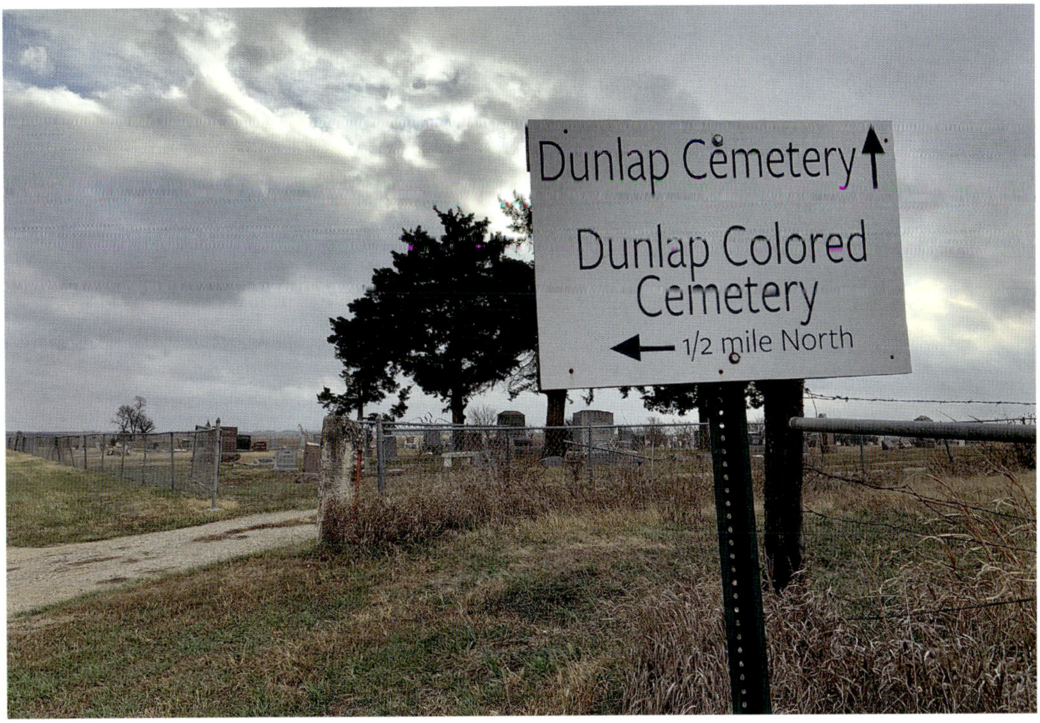

Sign for the Dunlap Cemetery, located 1.5 miles outside Dunlap, November 2020. Another half mile away is Dunlap's Colored Cemetery.

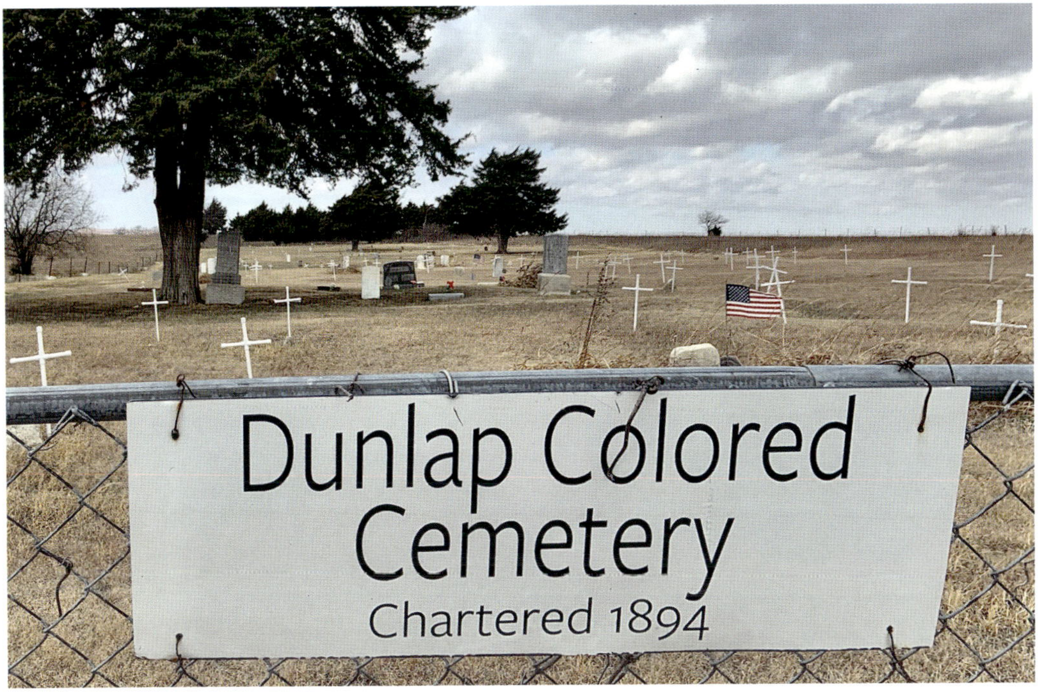

The Dunlap Colored Cemetery, November 2020. There are some headstones, but it was mostly unmarked graves. Now, those graves have crosses made of PCV piping.

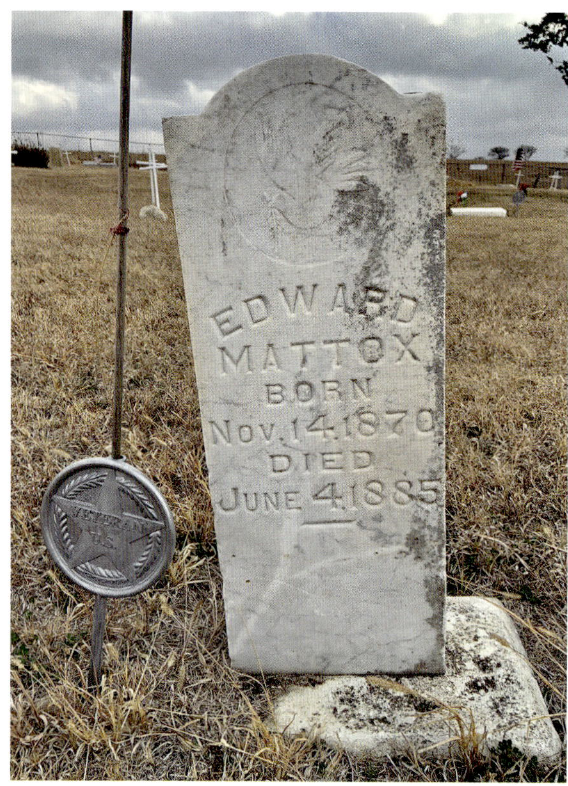

Headstone for Edward Mattox, November 2020. Born in 1870, he passed away at the age of fifteen and was buried in the colored cemetery five years after it was established.

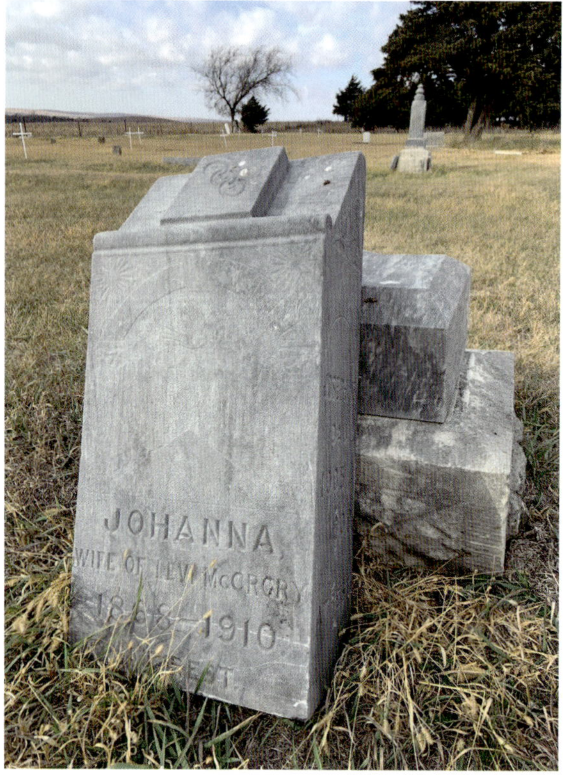

Headstone for Johanna McCrory, November 2020. Born in 1868, she passed away at the age of forty-two. She was the wife of Levi McCrory.

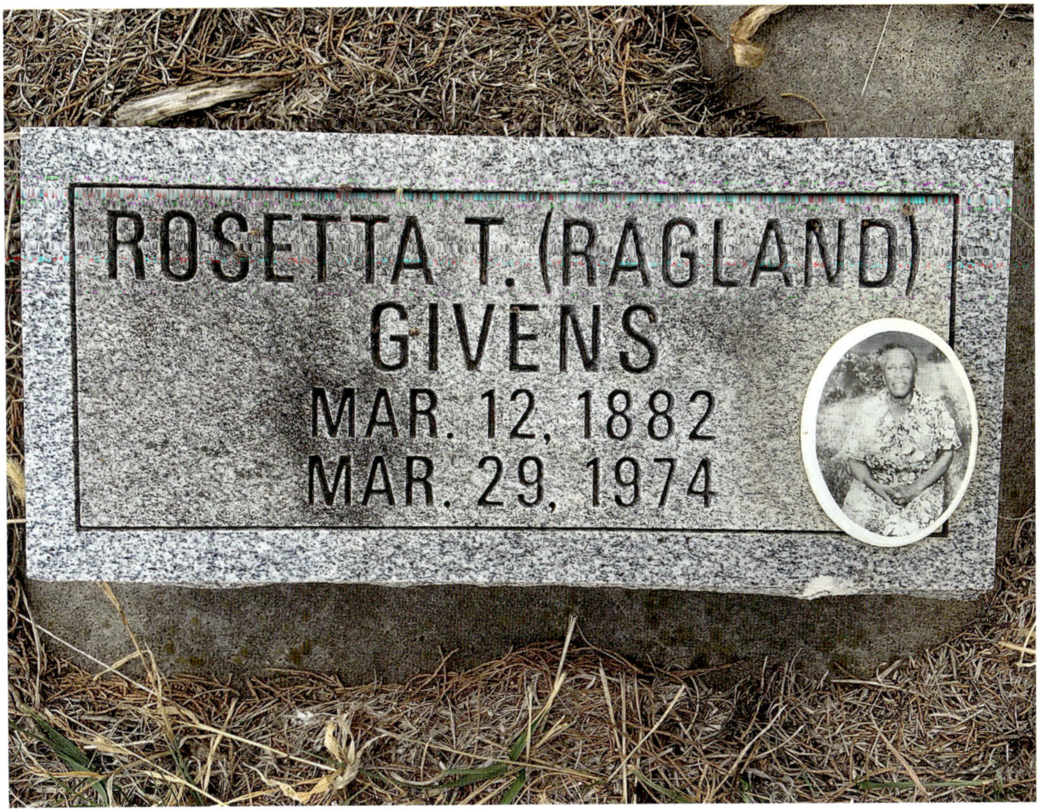

Above: Headstone for Rosetta Ragland-Givens, November 2020. Born in 1882, she passed away shortly after her ninety-second birthday. I love that her family put her photo on her headstone.

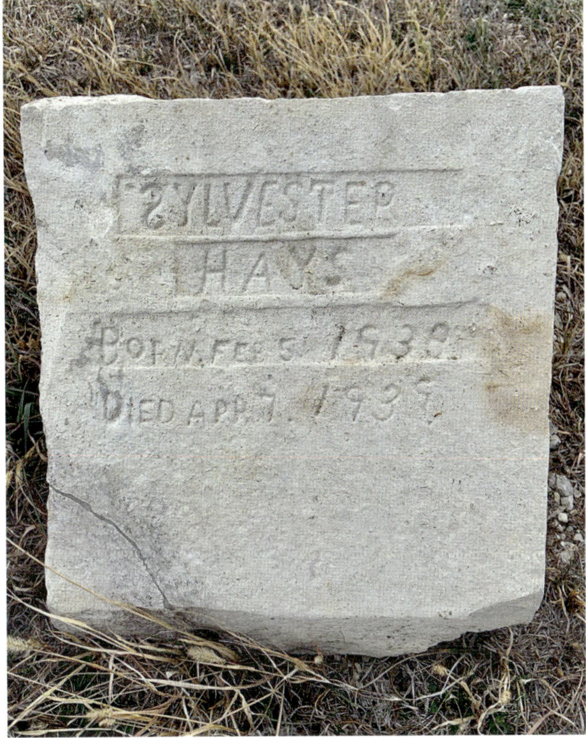

Right: Headstone for Sylvester Hays, November 2020. Born in 1938, he passed away one month after his first birthday. His stone was nearly unrecognizable until it was refurbished in 2019.

2

BUSHONG

Bushong Population: 33 (2019)

Another ghost town with a fascinating story is the town of Bushong. Like many of the small towns in Kansas, Bushong's modest beginnings start with being a train town that was originally known as Weeks, after Joseph Weeks, a local farmer who donated a portion of his land for the town's Missouri Pacific train station. The town would soon change the name to Bushong in 1886 after the catcher for the Major League Basketball's St. Louis Browns, Albert John "Doc" Bushong.

After earning a degree in dentistry at the University of Pennsylvania, he went on to be the catcher for the St. Louis Browns in the mid-1880s. During his time playing ball, it believed that Doc Bushong invented the cushioned catcher's mitt in an effort to keep his hands in good condition for when he would start practicing dentistry. His cushioned catcher's mitt is truly the epitome of the saying, "necessity is the mother of invention." He played for a total of five other teams throughout his baseball career and would retire in 1890. After retiring, Doc finally started practicing dentistry in the New Jersey/New York area until his death in 1908. Unfortunately, he never got to visit the town that was named after him.

As diverse and interesting as Doc's life was, I had wondered why the town of Weeks would rename the town after a man that had absolutely nothing to do with the town. I found two stories behind the name change. According to the Lyon County Historical Society, it was after the 1886's winning game over the Chicago White Stockings in the National League that the owner of the St. Louis Browns honored his players by having a western city named after each of his players. Yet the Society for American Baseball Research states that "the Missouri Pacific Railroad honored several of the St. Louis players by naming several of its stops in their honor." Either way, it was in honor of Doc Bushong's time as a catcher.

The town of Bushong would never see over 200 residents even in the town's prime. A series of unfortunate events would play into why the town never flourished. In 1894, twelve people would die from diphtheria within two days. Twelve people might not sound like a lot, but when you are talking about 100 to 150 people, that is around 10 percent of the town dying in two days. The historical society did not distinguish the ages of the twelve individuals that passed from diphtheria, but it was the leading cause of death in children from the first discovered case in 1880 to when the vaccine was made in the 1920s.

Another factor that caused many to move away was the drought brought on by the dry summers. Then a large fire in the 1920s would damage a few buildings in the downtown part of Bushong, in which those buildings were never rebuilt or restored. The Great Depression (1929–1939) only added financial strain and ruin to businesses and people, forcing doors to close and residents to seek opportunities elsewhere. As many locals moved away and fewer businesses stayed in town, this impacted the train service, as well. The need for service would decrease over the years and would finally stop in 1957. It was one thing after another that would push Bushong into the ghost town that it is today and has been for many years.

Bushong was an interesting ghost town. The whole town is about two to three blocks and is a goldmine of abandoned buildings, homes, and vehicles. Pulling up to the high school turned elementary school, there was a civil war reenactment going on in the field right across the street. No one seemed concerned with what I was doing, so I continued to the school for my photographic walk-through. The high school is the largest abandoned building in town. It was built in two phases, with the main part started as a four-room schoolhouse in 1918, later adding the gymnasium/auditorium in 1926. After a couple of county school consolidations in the 1950s and the change from a high school to teaching third and fourth grade, the school would finally close its doors in 1970. The town would continue to use the school for another few years after the school's closure, but it appears to have been empty for a number of years as well. Now the building is just a distant memory of its former state. The original four-room part of the school is gutted and the gym/auditorium part is collapsed in. It is completely unrecognizable as to what that part used to be—just a pile of wood and debris with three of the four walls still standing around it.

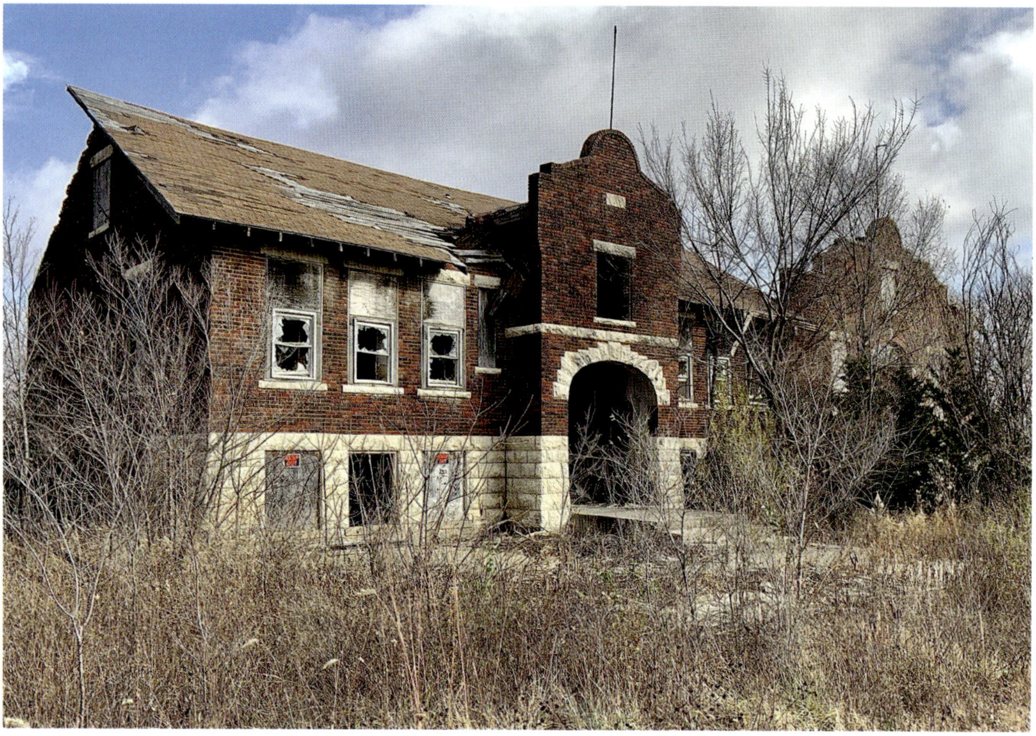

Front view of high school in Bushong, November 2020. It closed as a school in 1970.

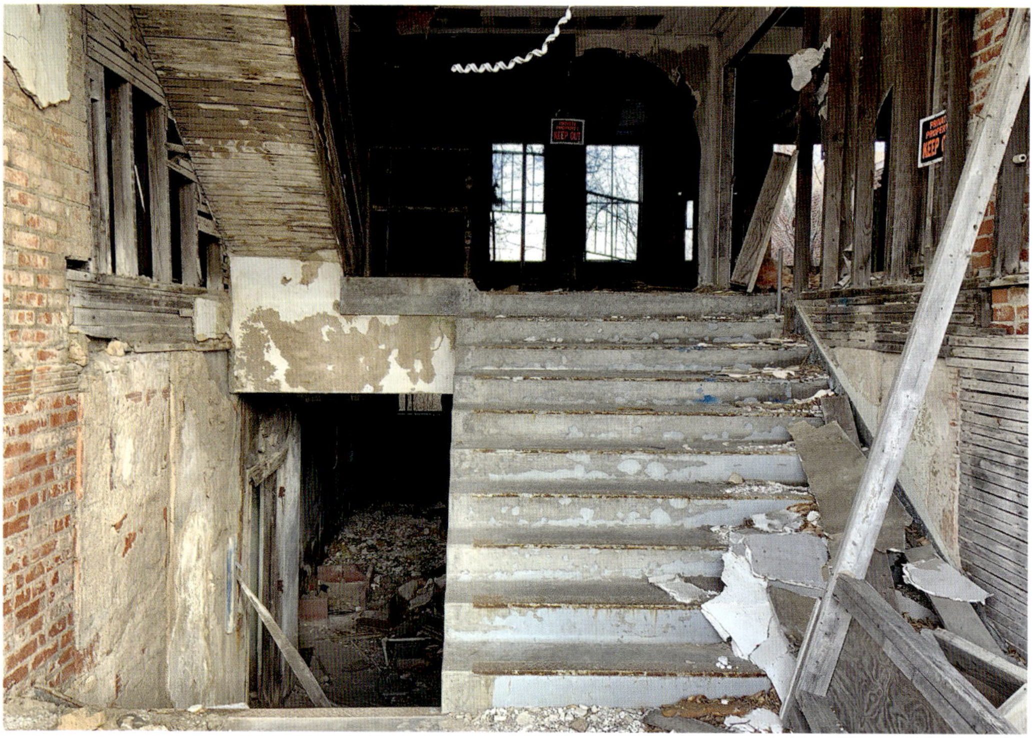

View of the main staircase, standing inside the front door arch of the high school, November 2020.

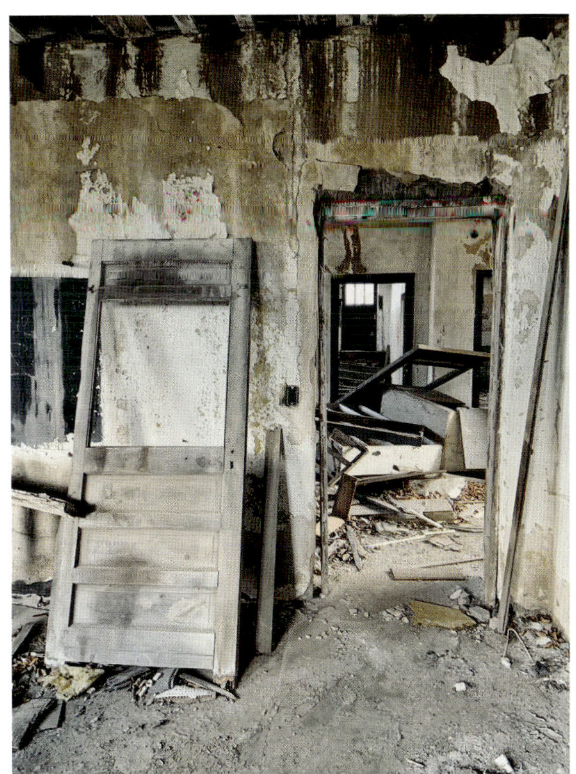

Right: In one of the classrooms on the bottom floor, looking down the hall inside the high school, November 2020.

Below: One of the gutted classrooms inside the former high school. The open door leads to the auditorium/gym that is now collapsed, November 2020.

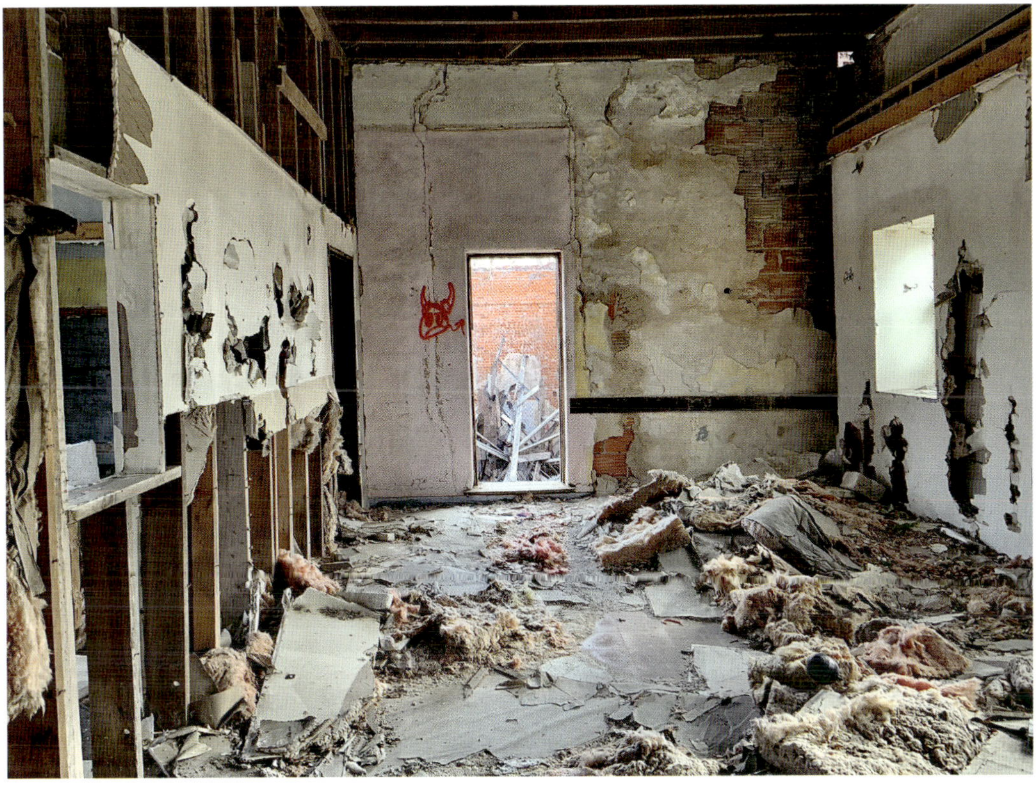

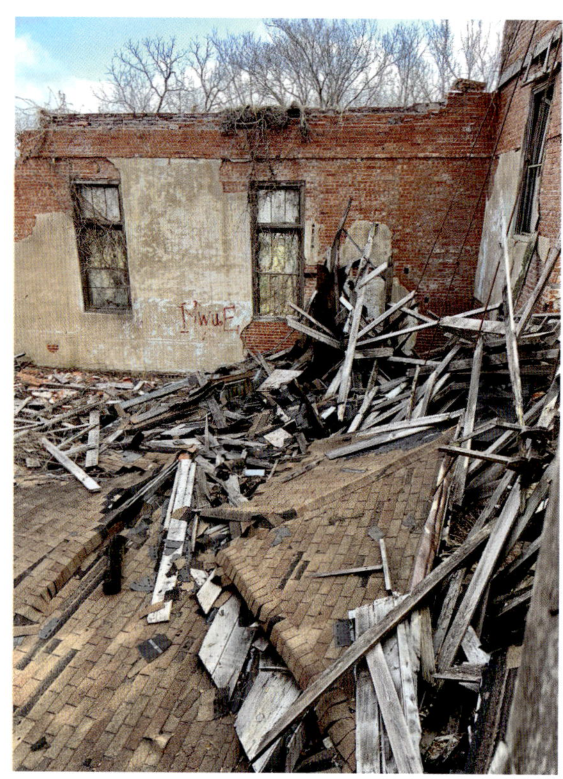

Left: View of collapsed auditorium/gym from the upstairs classroom inside the Bushong high school, November 2020.

Below: Outside view of the collapsed auditorium/gym side of the Bushong high school, November 2020.

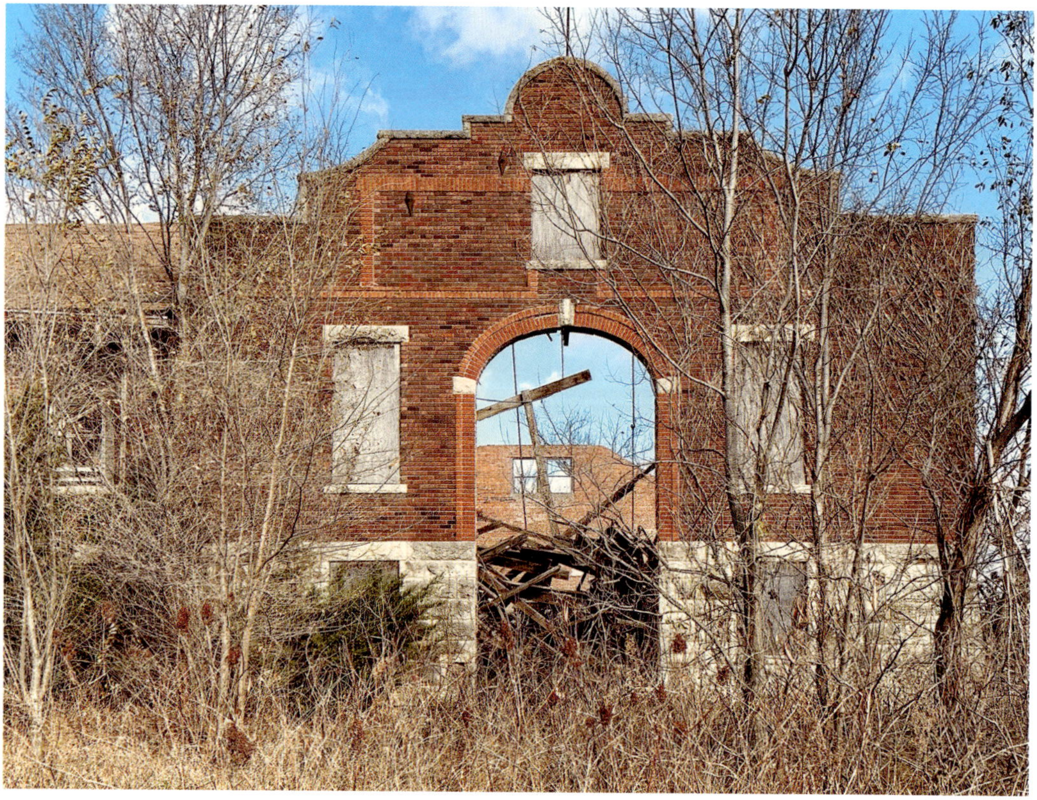

One block over from the school is the former Bushong Bank. Today, it is just a stone frame of a building. The old wooden window frames and the brick bank vault are rusty but both are still intact. Established in 1916, the bank would only serve the Bushong community for sixteen years before having to close its doors in 1932 because of economic failure due to the Great Depression.

In 2018, the bank was bought by a Kansas couple in hopes of converting the old building into a veteran's museum. The new owners had high hopes and big plans for the former bank; however, when I arrived in late 2020, no work had been started.

Looking through historic photos of the bank that the county historic society sent me, it reminded me of a bank you would see in a classic western. Sitting at one corner of a dirt road intersection, there were buildings on both sides in its early years. I imagined that it was the busiest block in town during its hay day. Now it is a lonely stone shell of a building, which has outlasted the surrounding buildings.

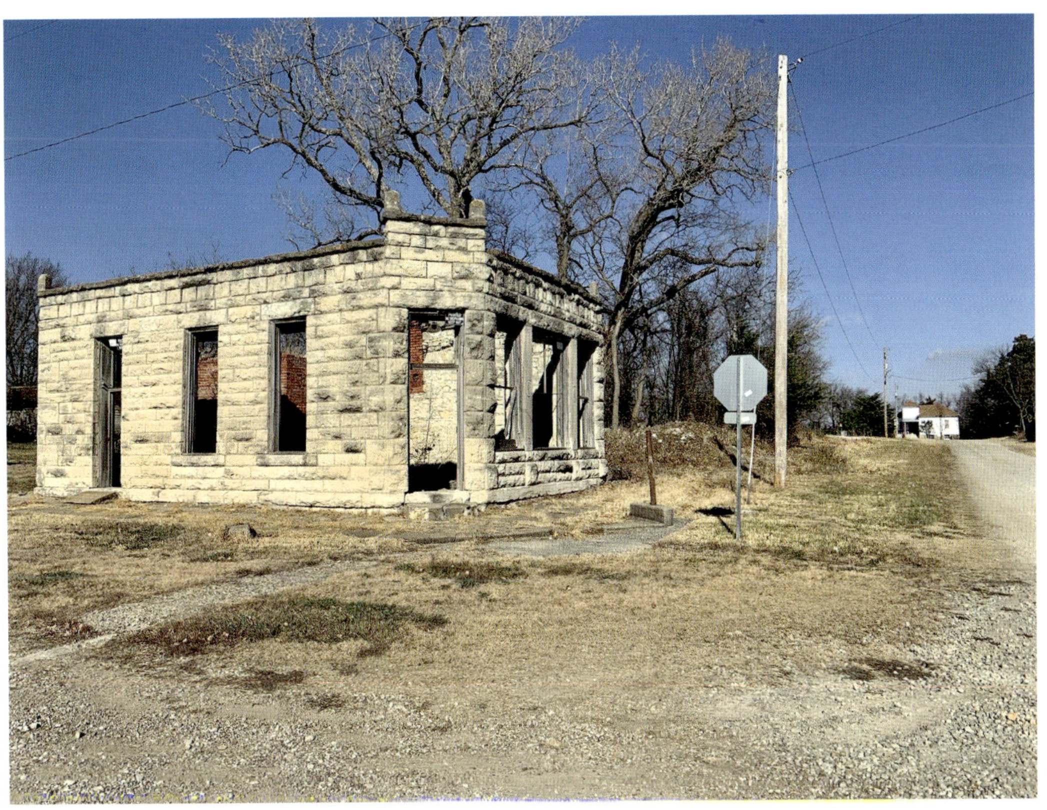

The former Bushong Bank is a stone shell building on the corner of Main and Third Street in Bushong, November 2020.

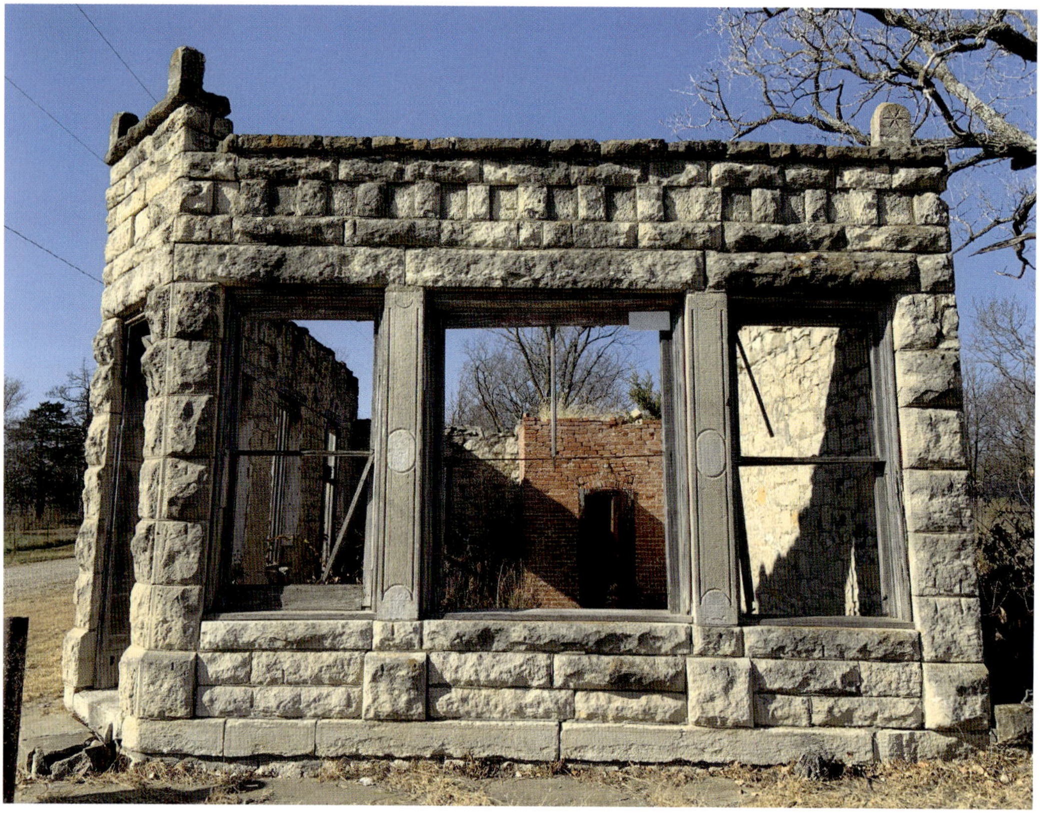

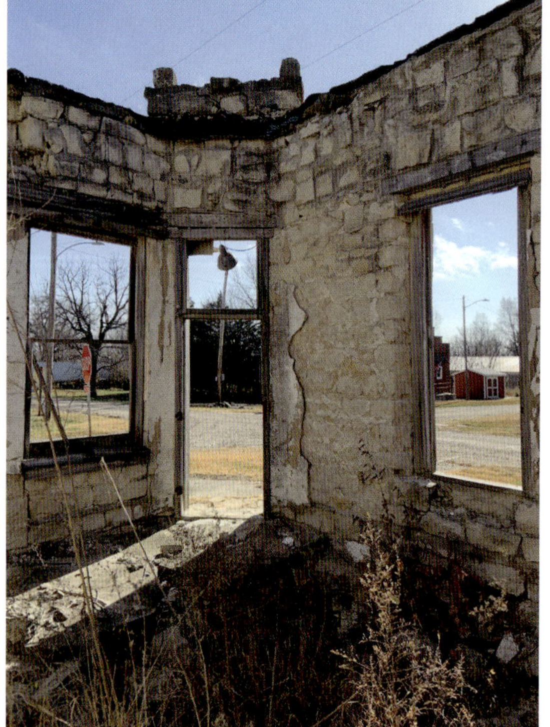

Above: Side view of the bank in Bushong, November 2020.

Left: Front door view from inside the bank building in Bushong, November 2020.

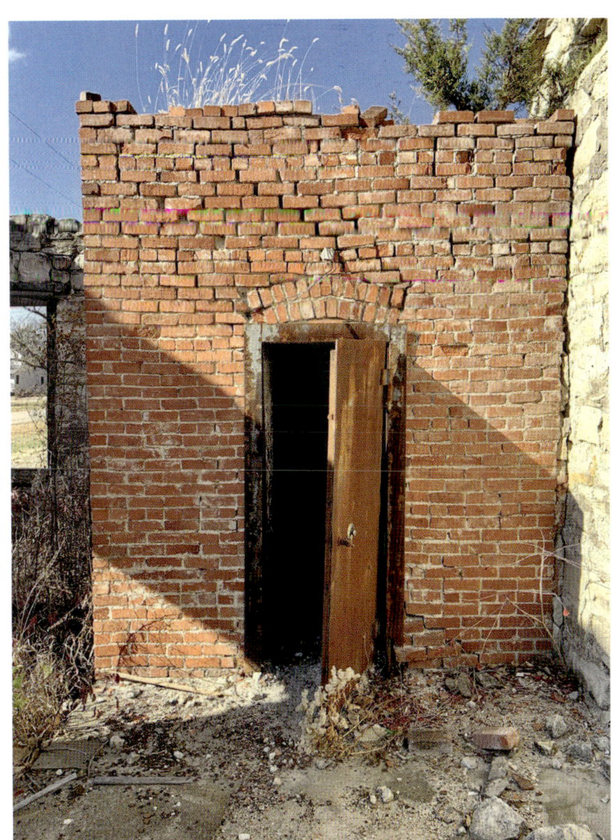

Right: The brick vault inside the former bank in Bushong, November 2020.

Below: The combination knob on the vault door in the bank in Bushong, November 2020.

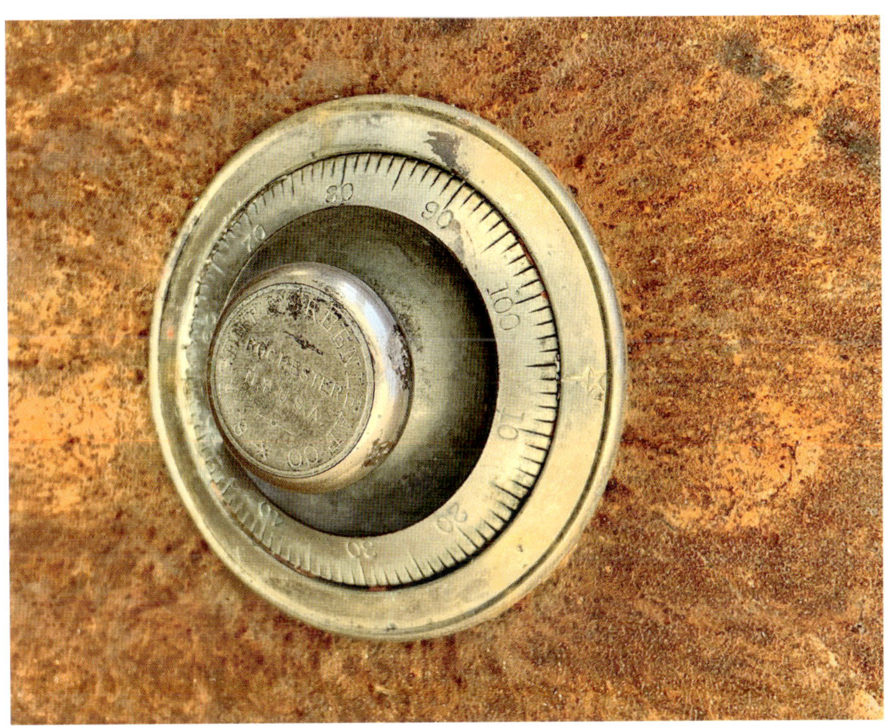

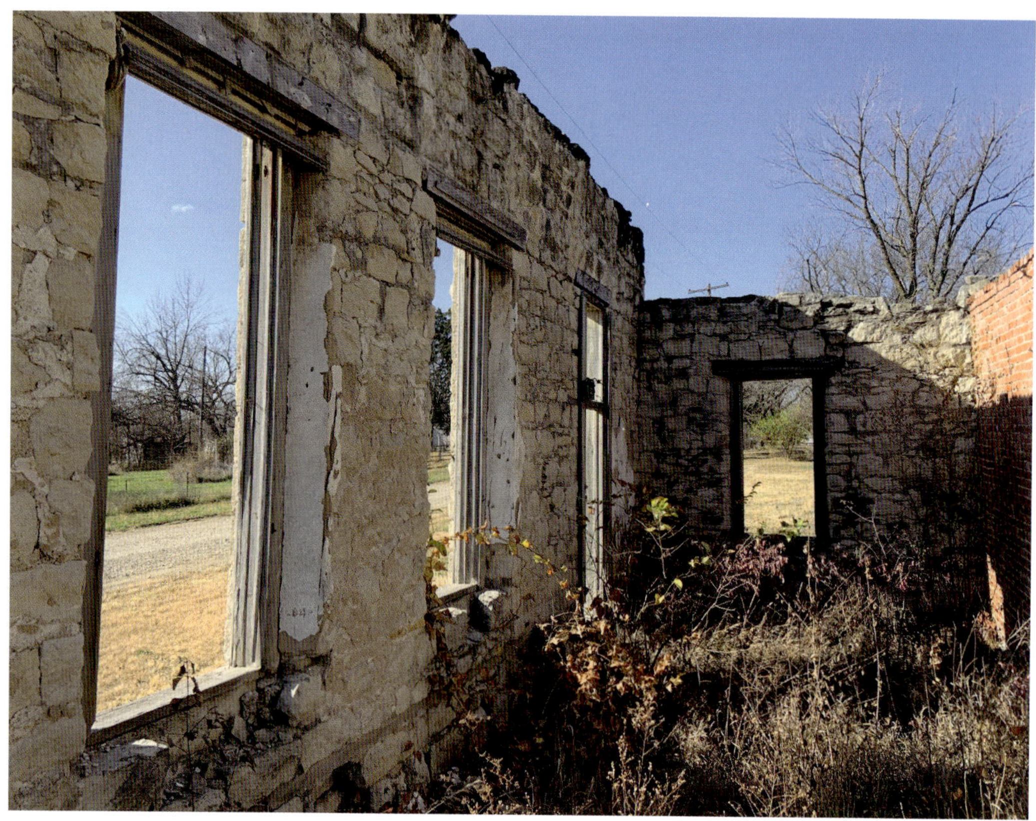

Inside the former bank building in Bushong, November 2020.

Just another block down the road was a multitude of the forgotten. All kinds of vehicles were left to rust in a couple of fields, the most interesting being an old passenger bus and a couple of deserted Volvos. The homes surrounding the cars and bus still had some personal possessions left behind. I like to look for dated items to give me approximate timelines of when the home or building was last used. Much of what was left behind was very dated, including a 1969 Book of the Year, a 1978 *Mork and Mindy* sticker on an old refrigerator, some 1993 family photos, and the 1995 registration sticker on one of the Volvo's license plates. It really was like time stopped once all this stuff had been abandoned and I was walking through a time capsule of what was left behind.

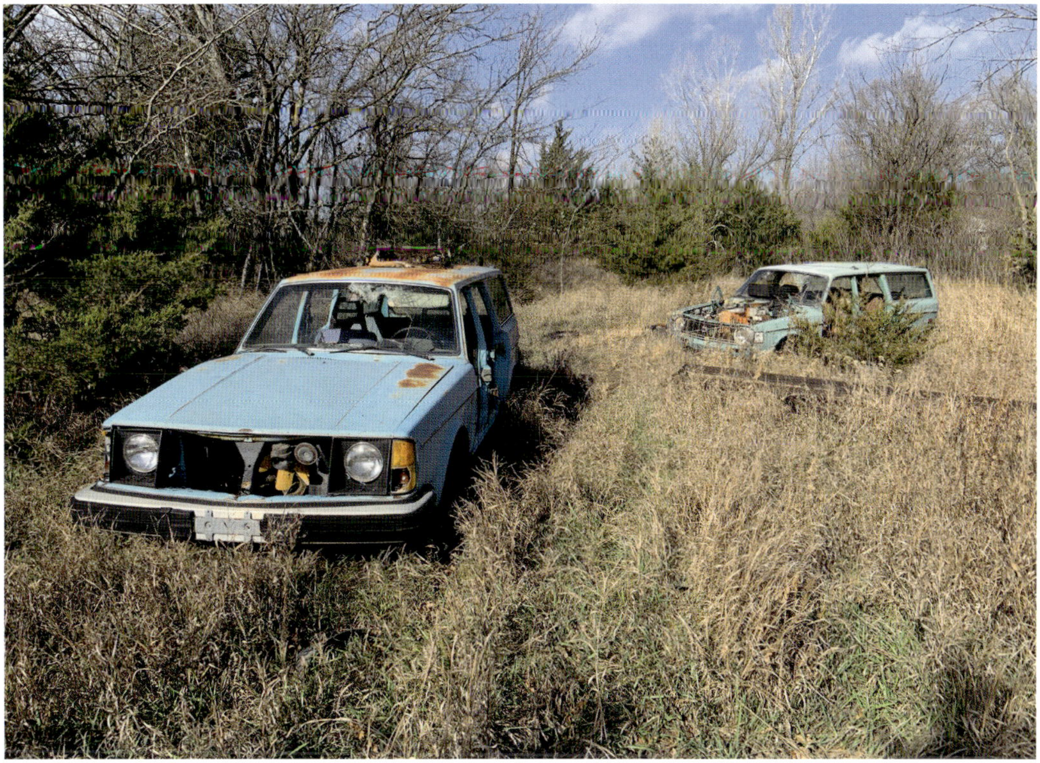

Abandoned Volvos in a field in Bushong, November 2020.

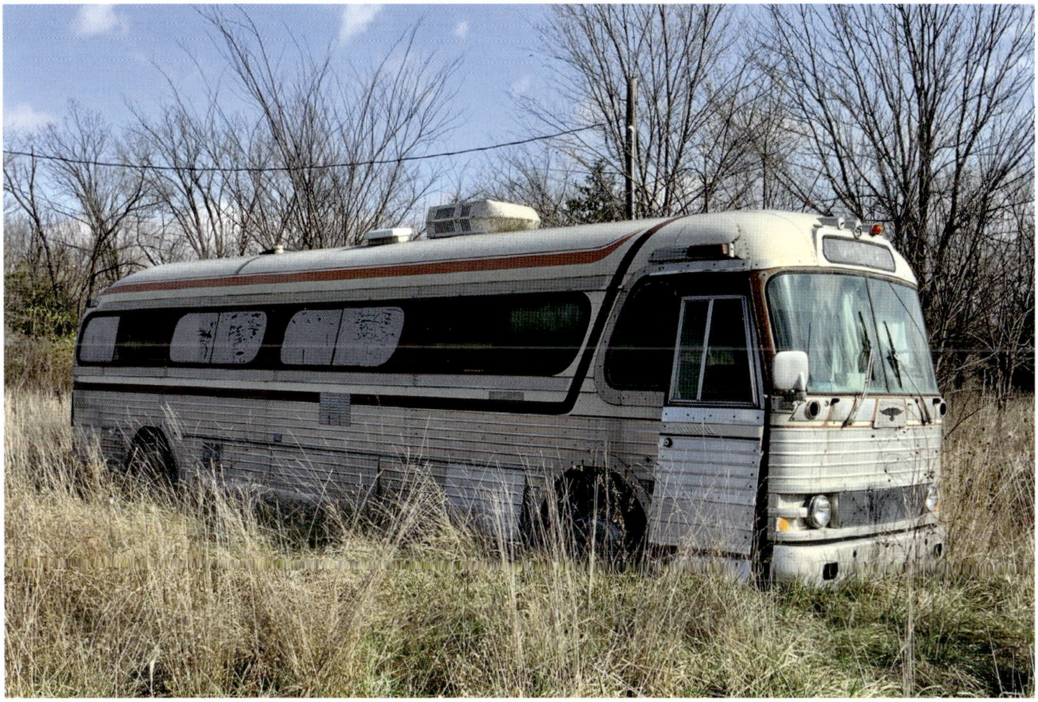

Abandoned bus in a field in Bushong, November 2020.

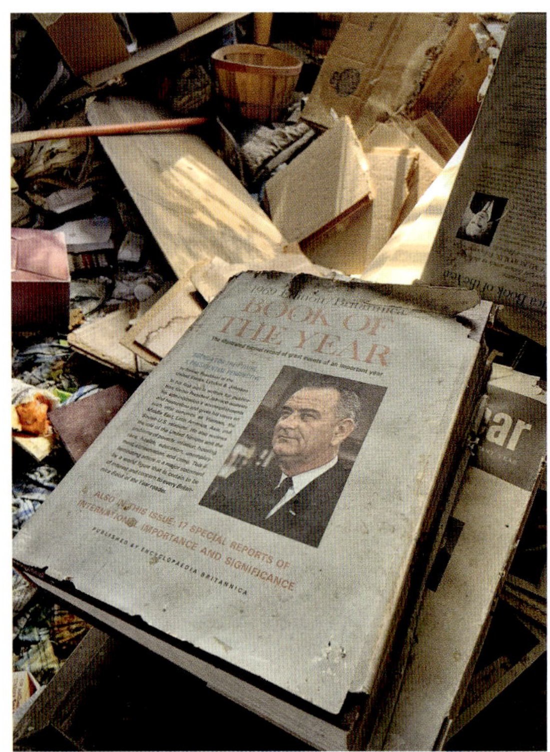

Left: The 1969 Book of the Year found on a counter in an abandoned trailer in Bushong, November 2020.

Below: A 1978 *Mork and Mindy* sticker on a refrigerator in an abandoned trailer in Bushong, November 2020.

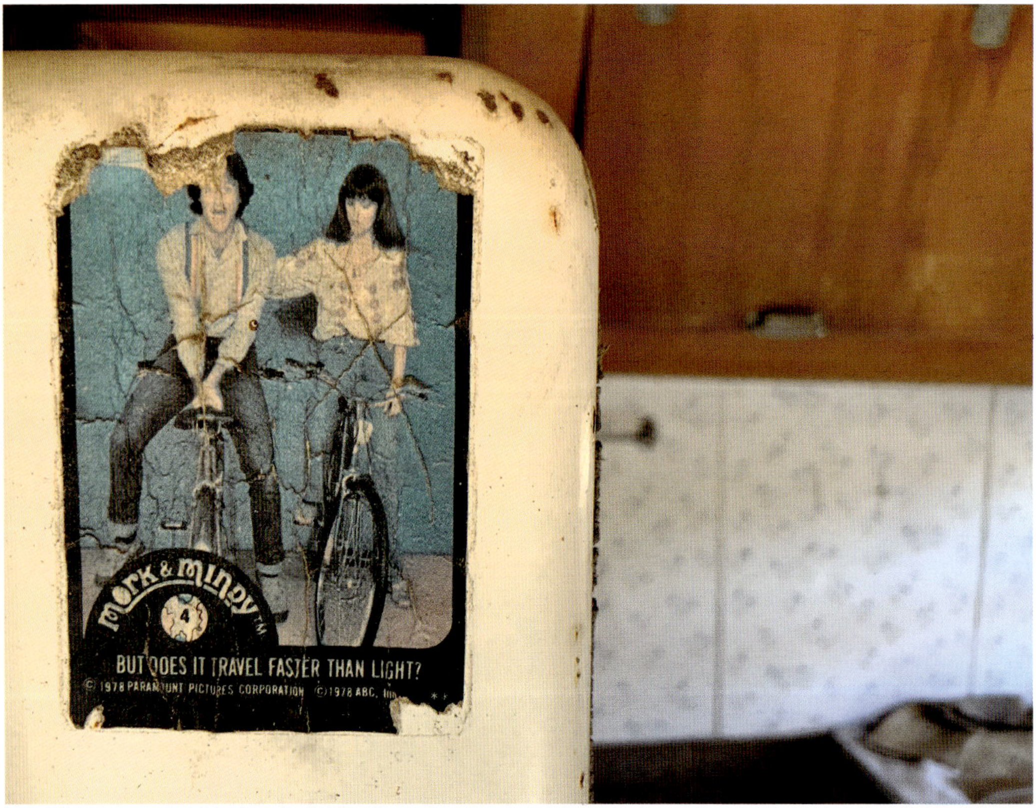

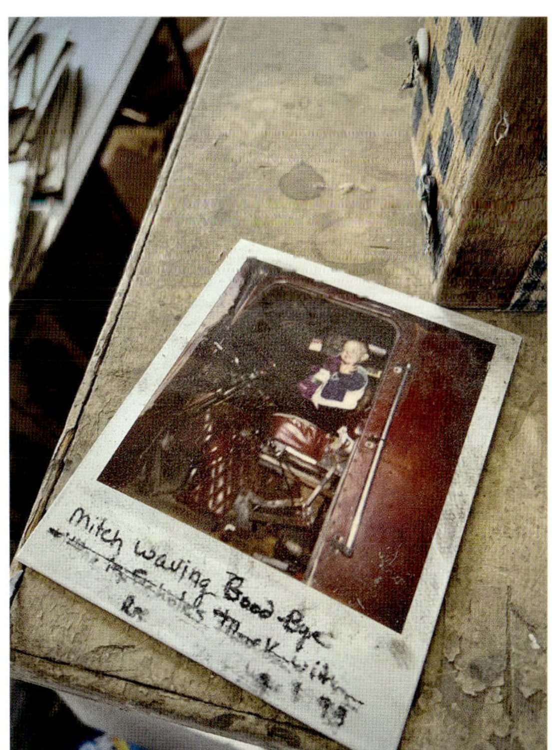

Right: A family photo from 1993 found in an abandoned trailer in Bushong, November 2020.

Below: The license plate on this abandoned Volvo, expired in November 1995. There is an abandoned bus in the field across the street in Bushong, November 2020.

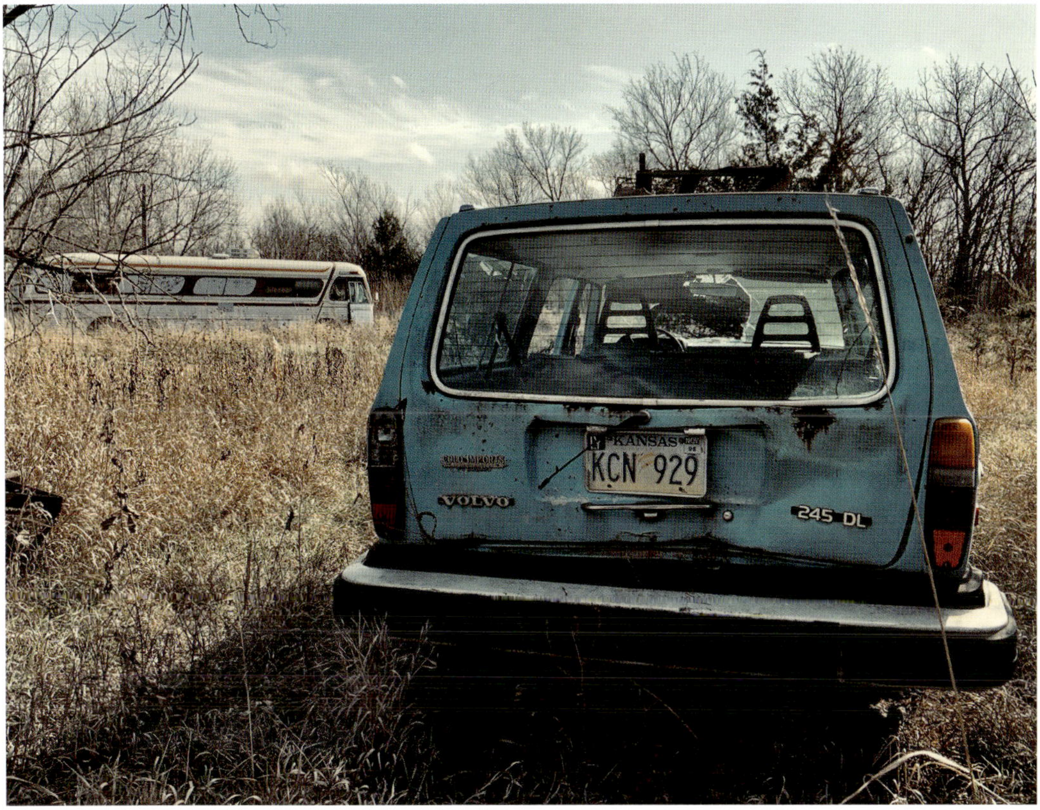

3

ELMDALE

Elmdale Population: 28 (2019)

Like many of the small towns throughout Eastern Kansas, Elmdale is similar in many regards—small in area, declining population, and many of the remaining buildings have fallen into serious disrepair. Established as a railroad town, the Atchison, Topeka, and Santa Fe Railway started going through Elmdale in 1871. Elmdale would see its highest population of around 250 people in the early part of the 1900s.

Over the years, Elmdale would face hit after hit starting with the Great Flood of 1951. That forced a lot of people to move away, but following the devastation, the town had a levy built to prevent future flooding. The bank and schools would close in the late 1960s, sending the few remaining students to a neighboring consolidated school. Finally, in 1998, floodwaters would rise over the town's levy, leaving much of the town beyond repair and fewer than 100 residents behind.

Today, Elmdale is block after block of the forgotten—houses, trailers, cars, and the school all just sitting, slowly decaying until they are either reclaimed by the nature around them or until their structures are so old and neglected that they fall in on themselves. While photographing the town, there were obvious signs that there were a few people still living here. However, I did not encounter or even see another person in the whole town. The post-apocalyptic vibe put off by the lack of people is a reoccurring theme throughout many ghost towns and it was no different here. It puts out the questioning mindset of, "Did I just miss everyone or are they all hiding?" The silence throughout the town added to the feeling of isolation—no vehicle sounds off in the distance, no noise that can come from people doing outdoor activities, not even any animal noises, just a level of quiet that you never hear when you live in the city. I left Elmdale as quietly as I came, leaving it as I found it, frozen in time.

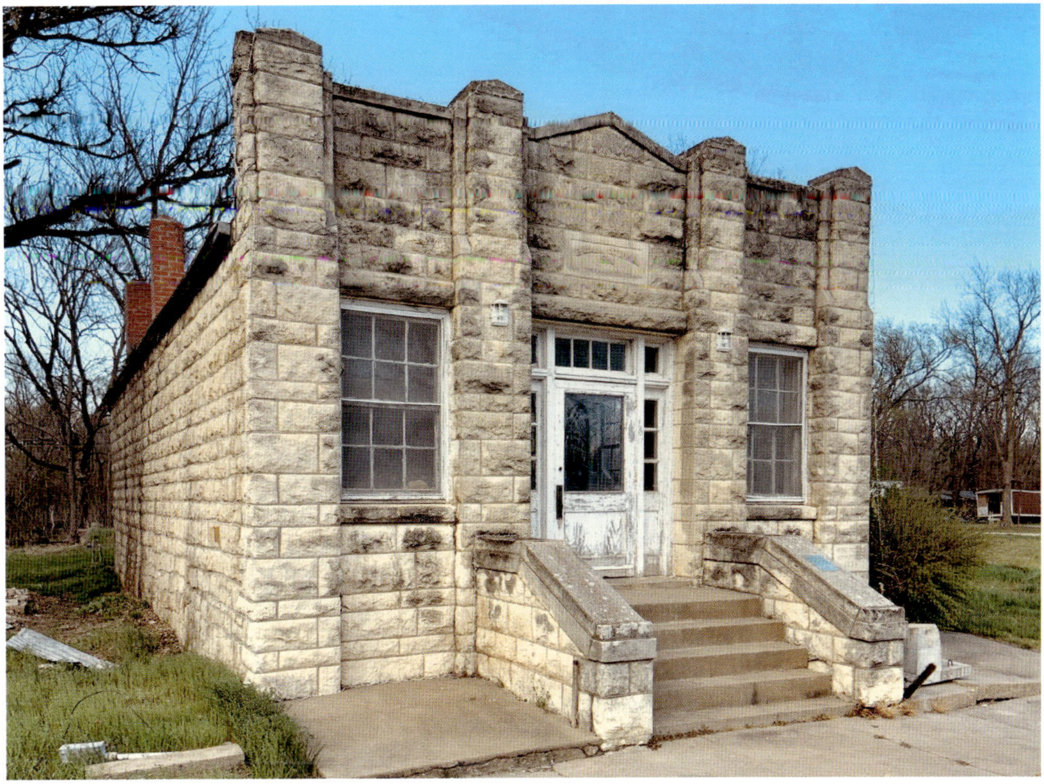

Elmdale City Hall, April 2020.

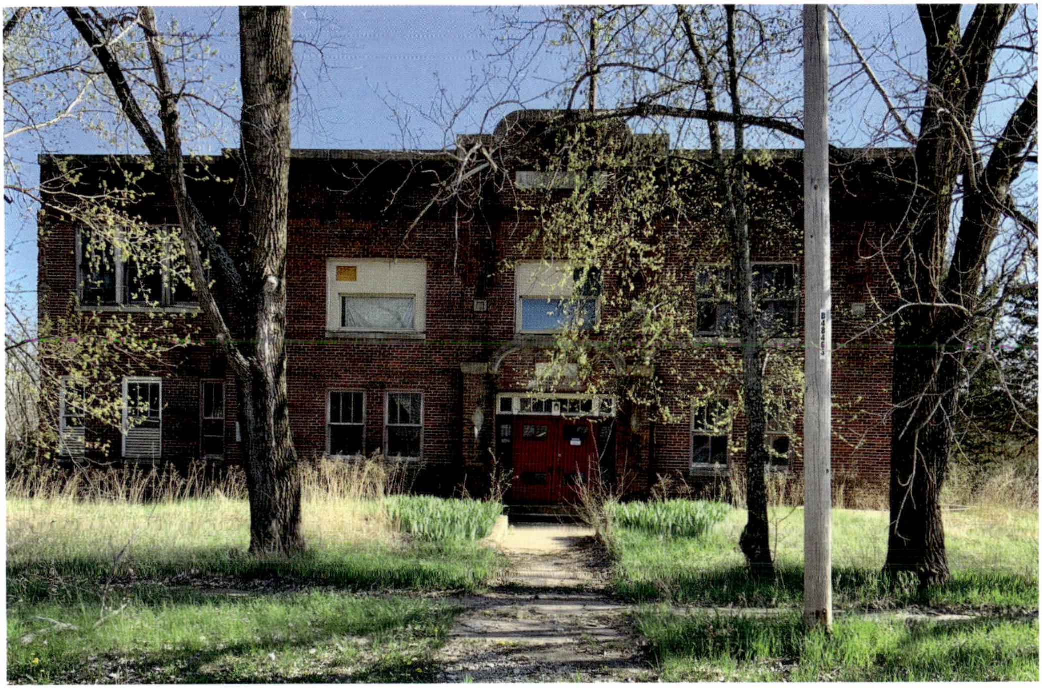

School in Elmdale, April 2020.

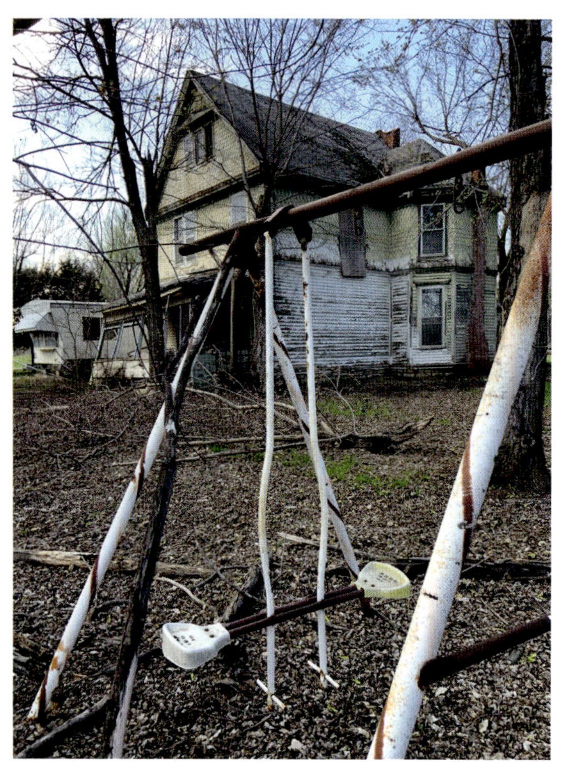

Left: Abandoned house, trailer, and swing set in Elmdale, April 2020.

Below: Abandoned house and RV in Elmdale, April 2020.

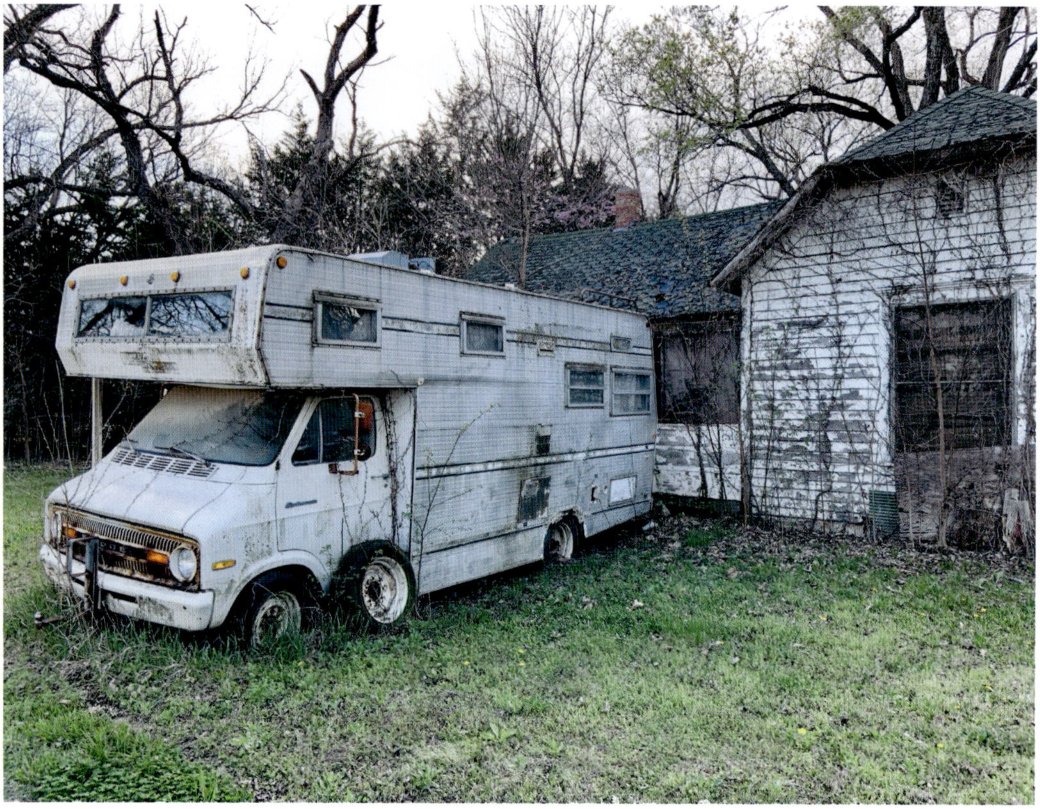

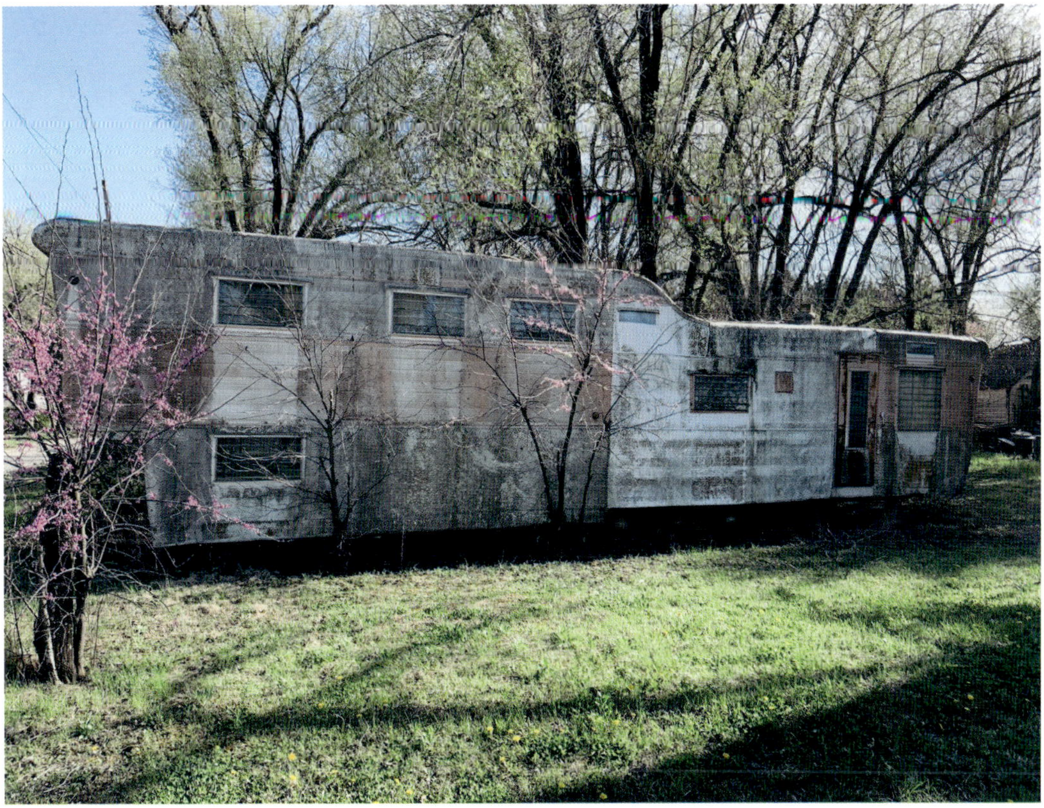

Above: Abandoned trailer in Elmdale, April 2020.

Right: Abandoned van and engine in Elmdale, April 2020.

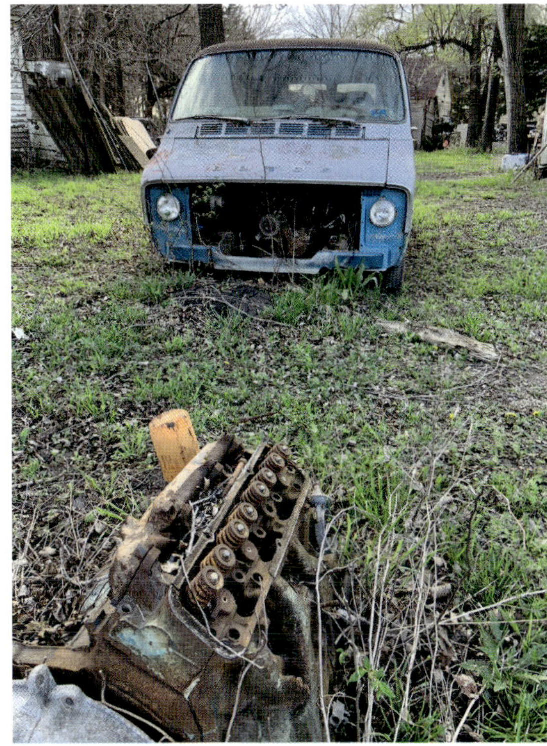

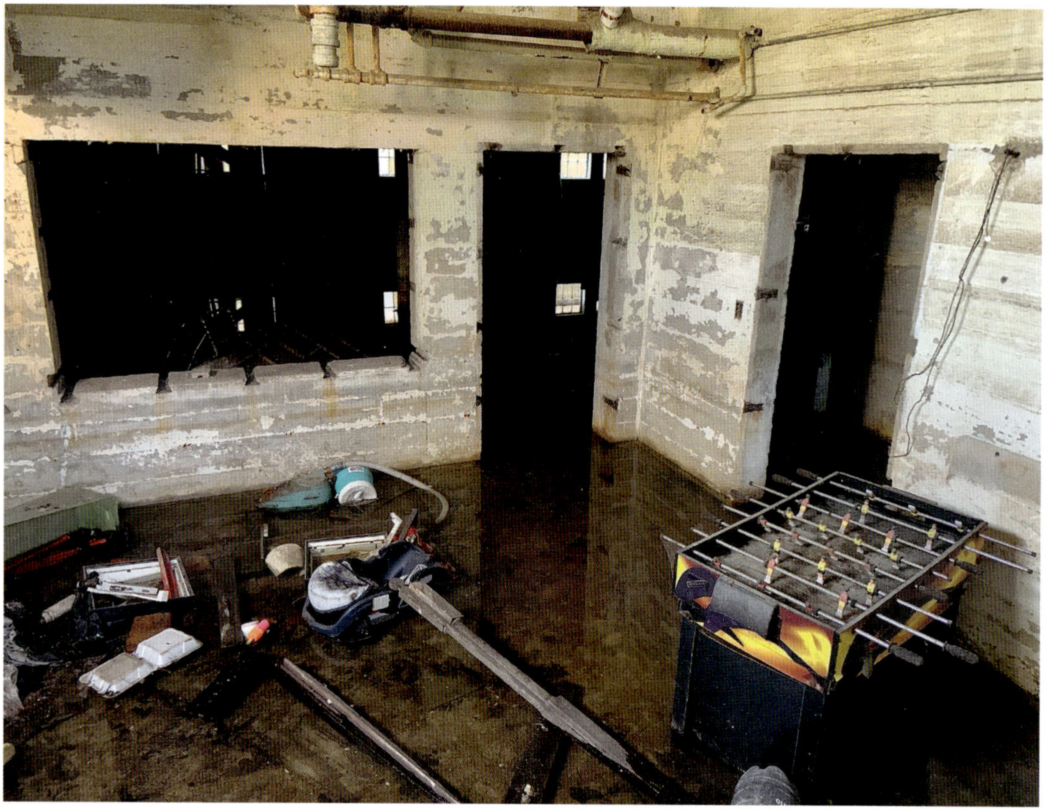

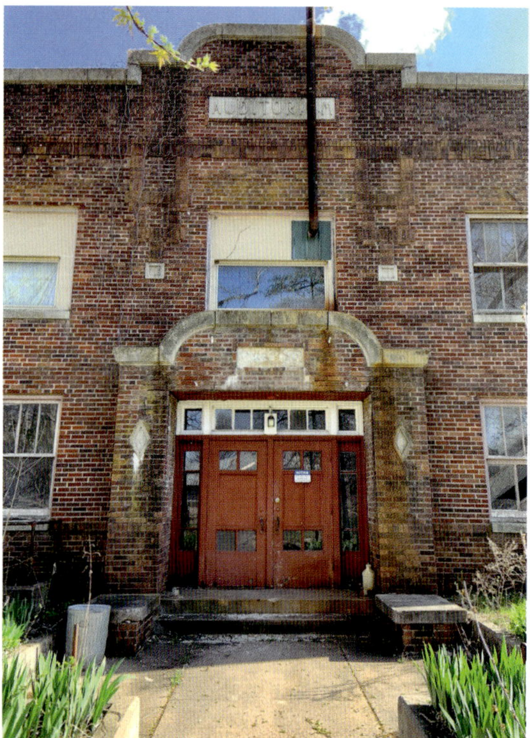

Above: The basement is flooded at the school in Elmdale, April 2020.

Left: Front of the school in Elmdale, April 2020.

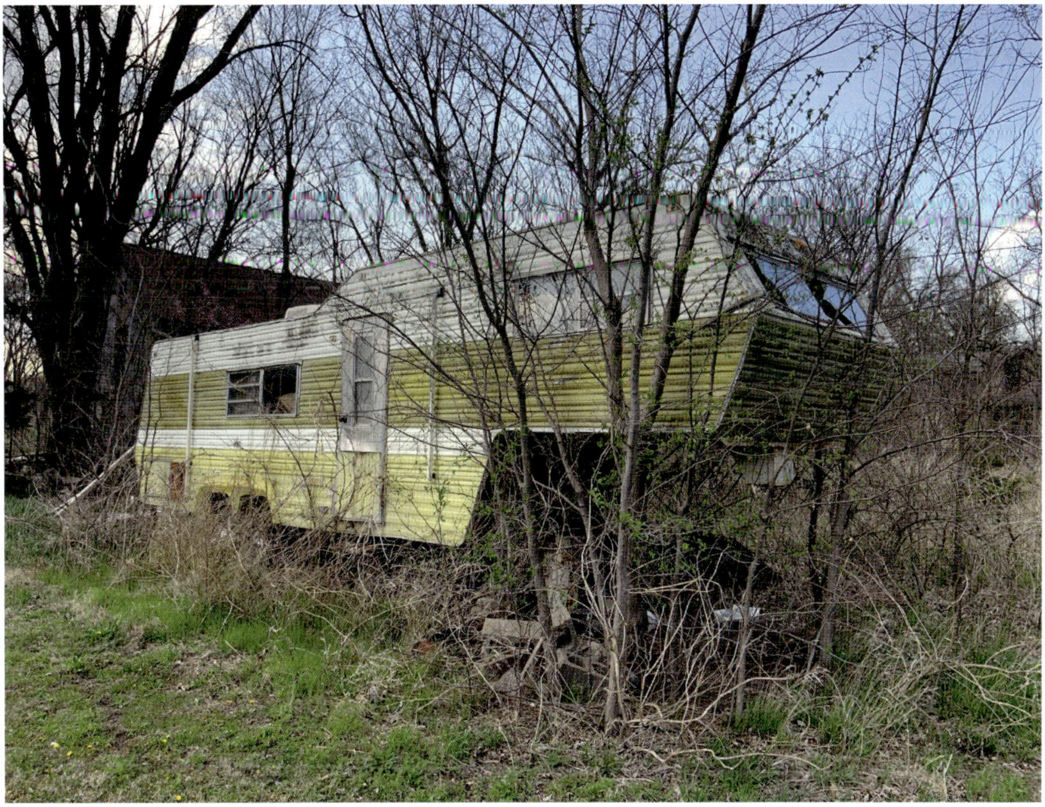

Above: Another abandoned trailer in Elmdale, April 2020.

Right: Abandoned house and trailer in Elmdale, April 2020.

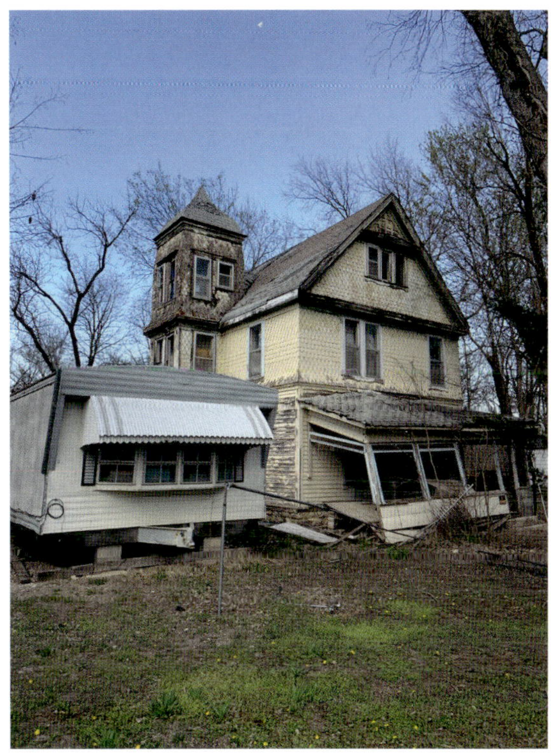

4

CEDAR POINT

CEDAR POINT POPULATION: 27 (2019)

Founded in 1862, Cedar Point (like many towns of the area) experienced a slight influx of residents in the first few decades, followed by a steady decline to the small population that it is today. As residents have moved away, the town started its decline. Small schools eventually consolidated to a bigger nearby town, empty houses fell into disrepair, and the town's businesses did not make enough money to keep the doors open. Currently, much of Cedar Point is abandoned and falling apart. The school has mostly collapsed in, leaving just the brick exterior and gymnasium side of the school intact. Despite the damage and not being used for a number of years, there are still school trophies in the display case and all of the library books lay in rows on the floor in one of the rooms upstairs. Many of the town's businesses are closed, leaving the town's roads lined up with empty buildings.

The Cedar Point Mill that sits on the Cottonwood River as you enter town went from being "the largest mill in Chase County" to an empty, deteriorating building. Cedar Point's most notable building was built in 1867 and was originally made of wood. Over the years, everything about the mill would change, from the name change to Drinkwater and Schriver Mill in 1870 to constructing a bigger mill made of stone, completed in 1875.

Today, the old mill has cracks on all sides of the foundation and walls. The different owners have taken efforts to repair the mill over the years, but despite their best efforts, that has not stopped the continued declension. Without some much-needed attention and maintenance, it is safe to say that the Drinkwater and Schriver Mill is going to crumble into the river. I hope that the mill does not succumb to the same fate as much of the town that surrounds it.

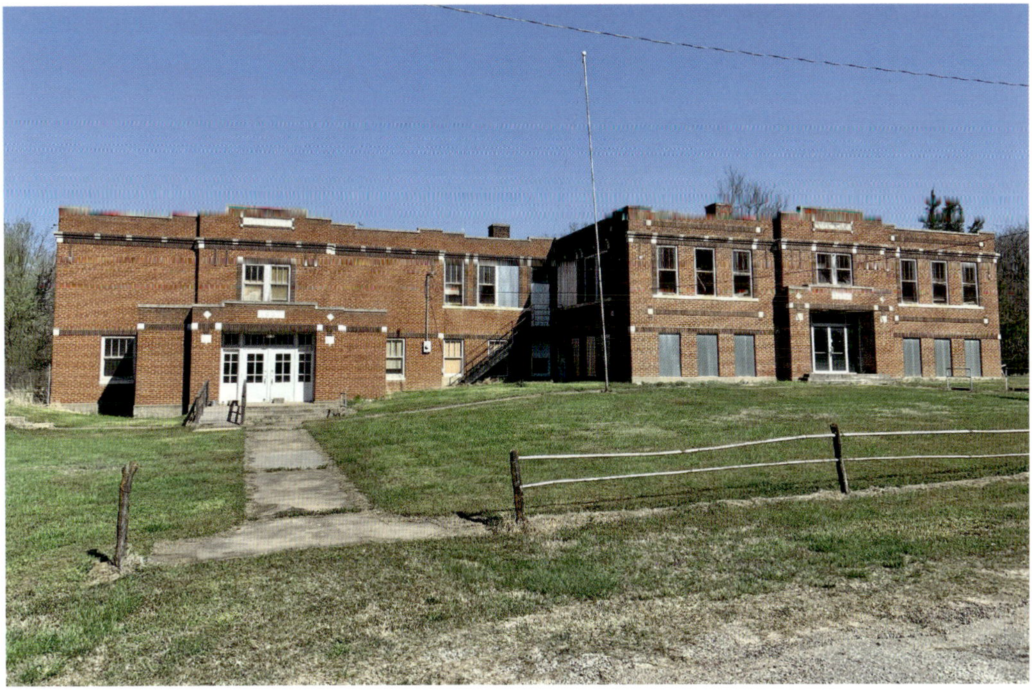

Front view of the school in Cedar Point, April 2020.

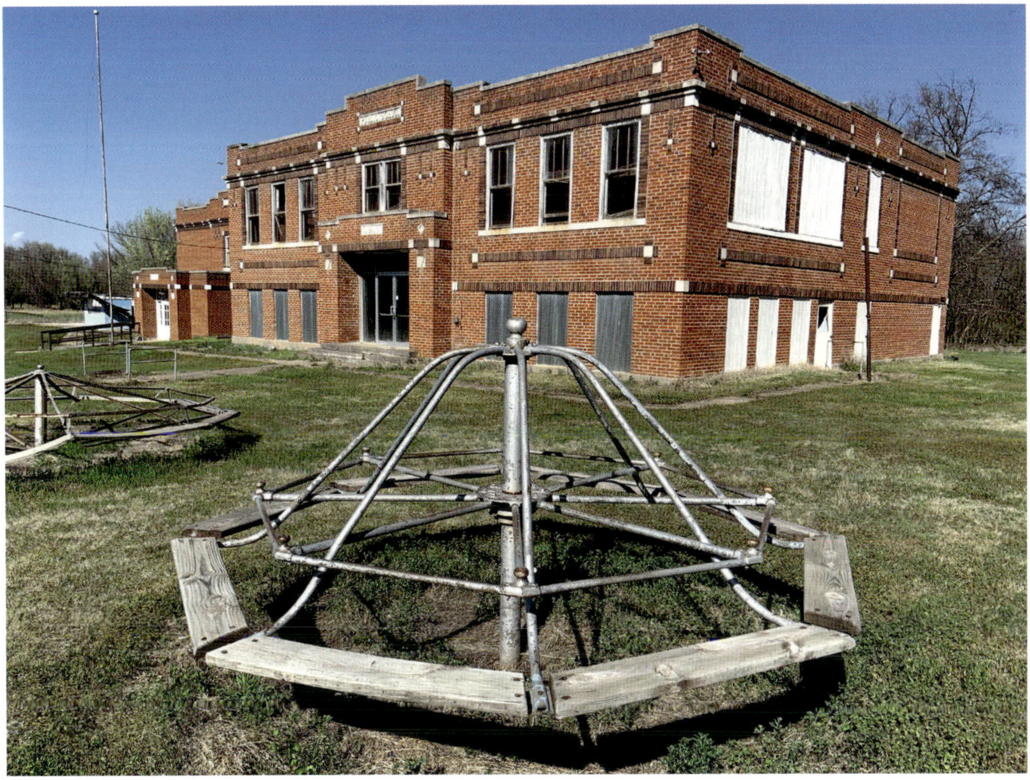

Abandoned school in Cedar Point, April 2020.

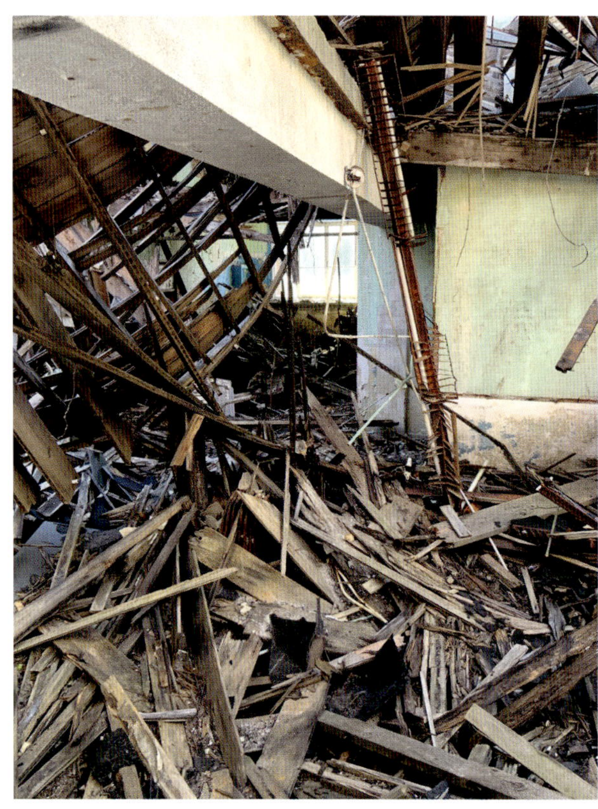

Left: Collapsed part in an abandoned school in Cedar Point, April 2020.

Below: Gymnasium/auditorium in an abandoned school in Cedar Point, April 2020.

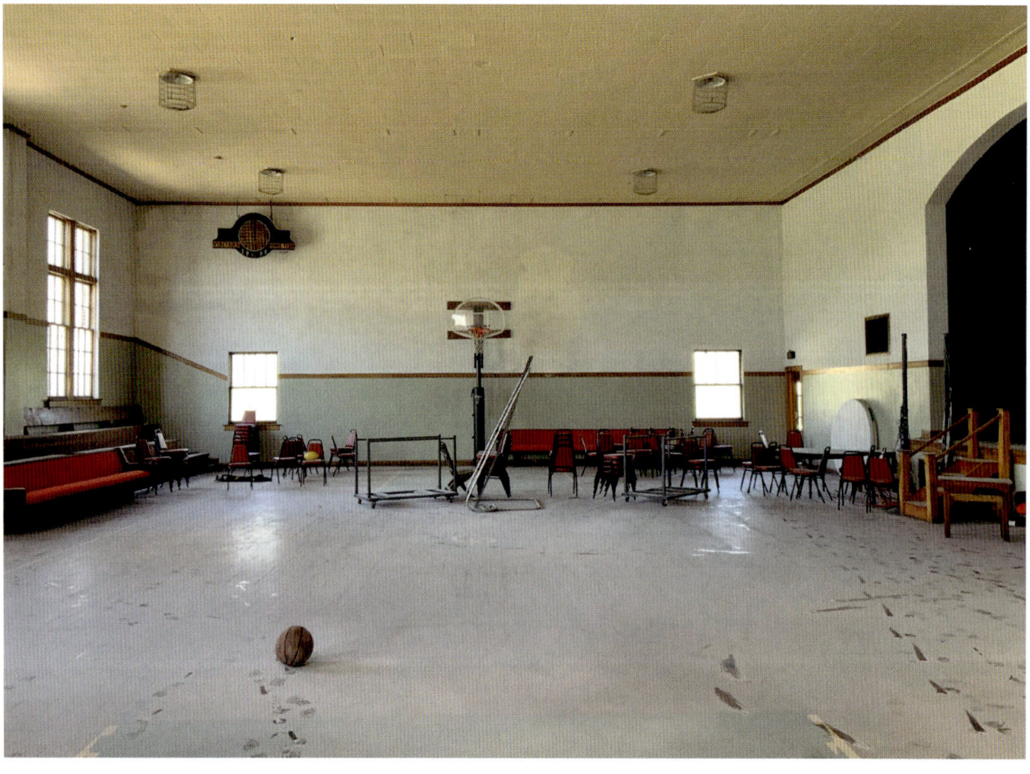

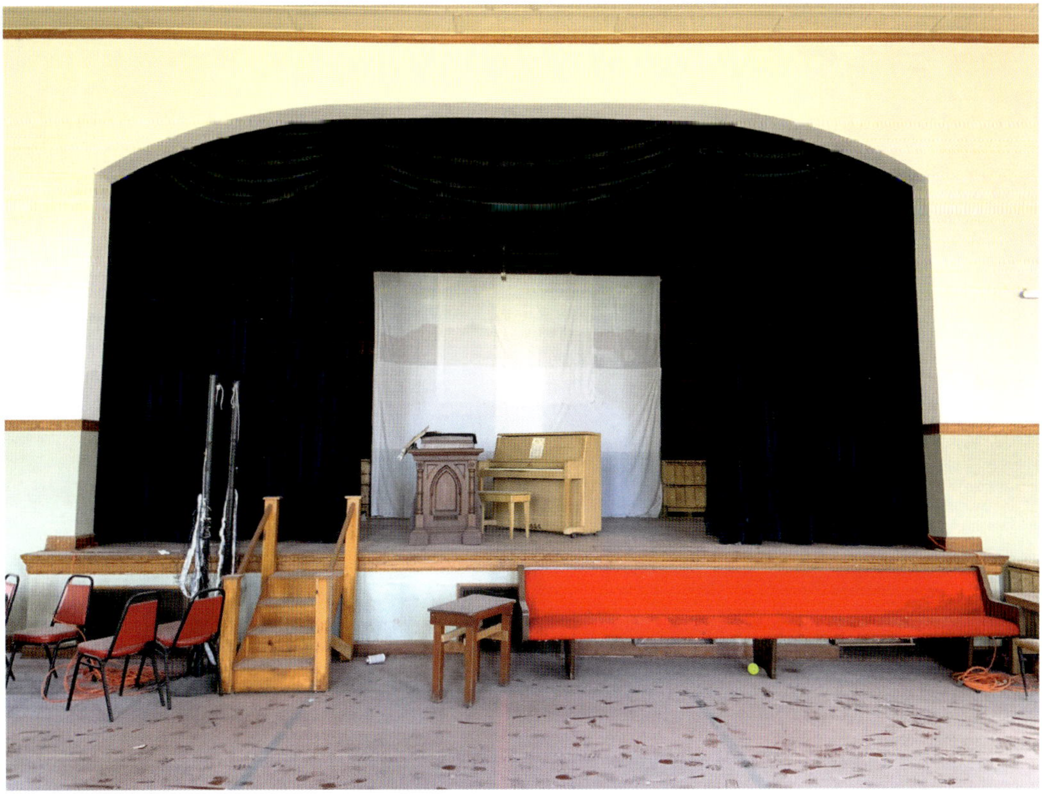

Above: Auditorium stage in an abandoned school in Cedar Point, April 2020.

Right: Books all over the table and floor in this classroom in an abandoned school in Cedar Point, April 2020.

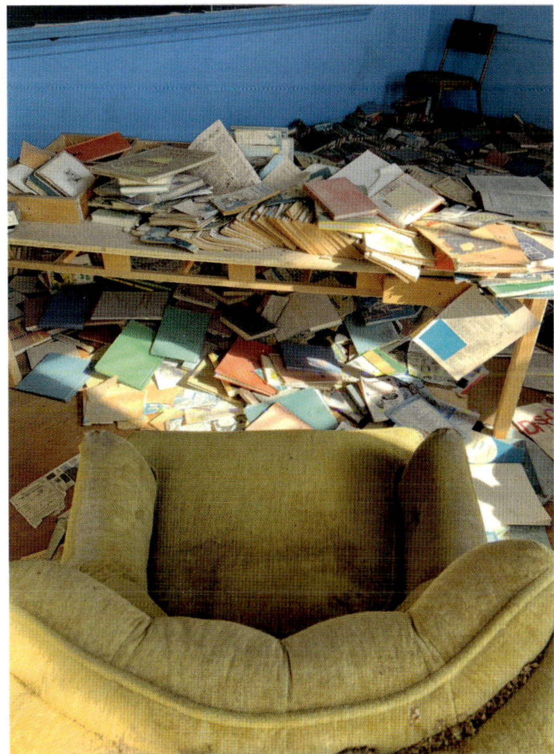

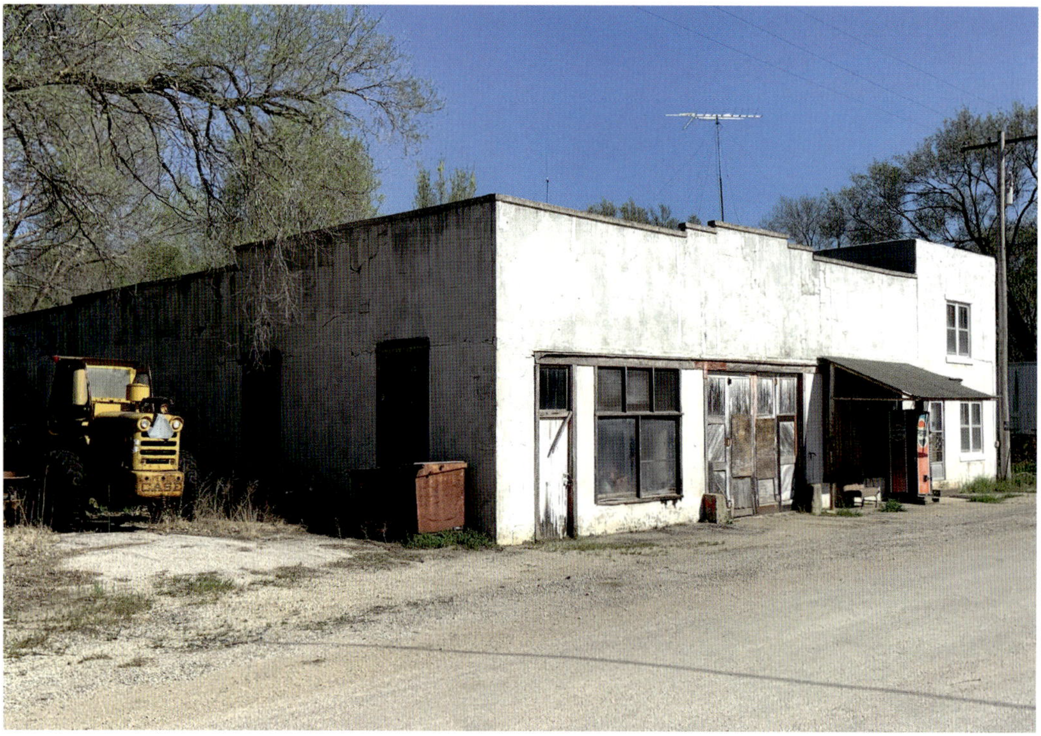

Abandoned building and tractor in Cedar Point, April 2020.

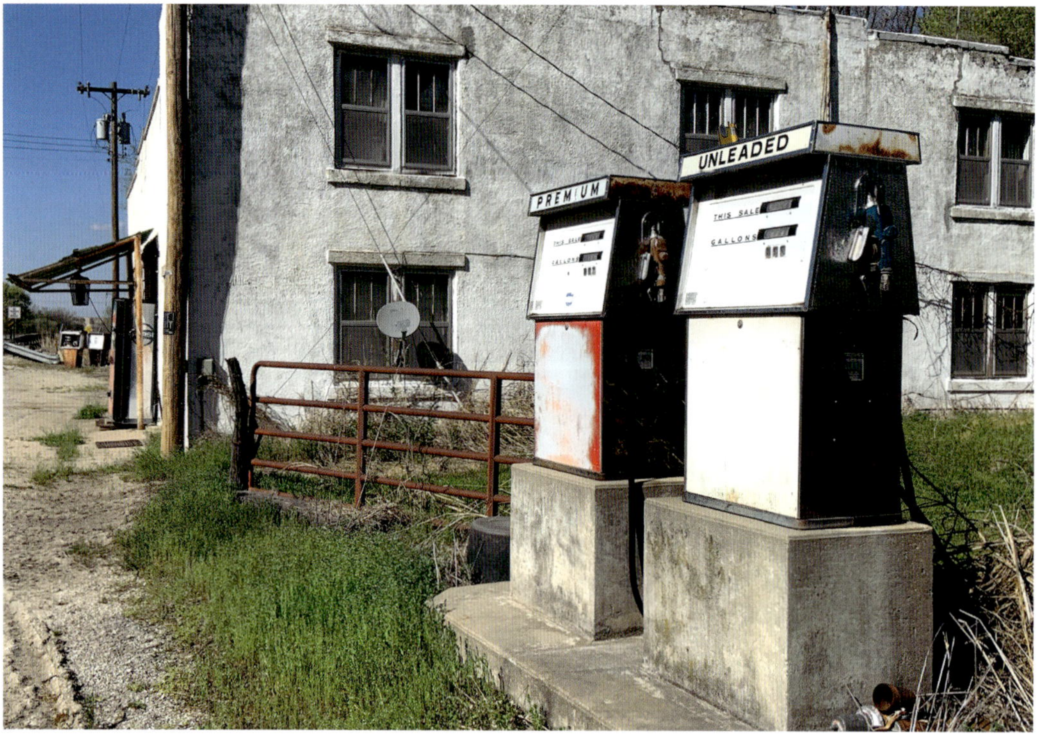

Non-functioning gas pumps sit outside an abandoned building in Cedar Point, April 2020.

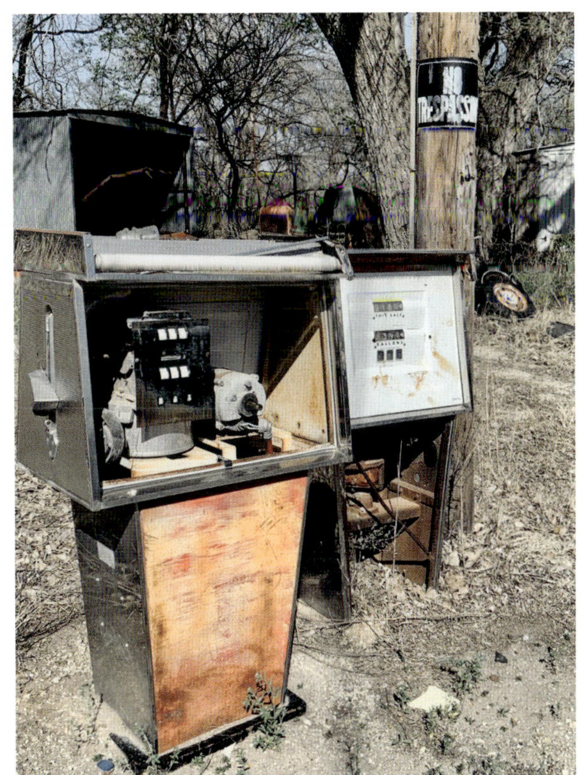

Right: More old gas pumps sit rusting outside an abandoned building in Cedar Point, April 2020.

Below: Back of the Drinkwater and Schriver Mill on the Cottonwood River in Cedar Point, April 2020.

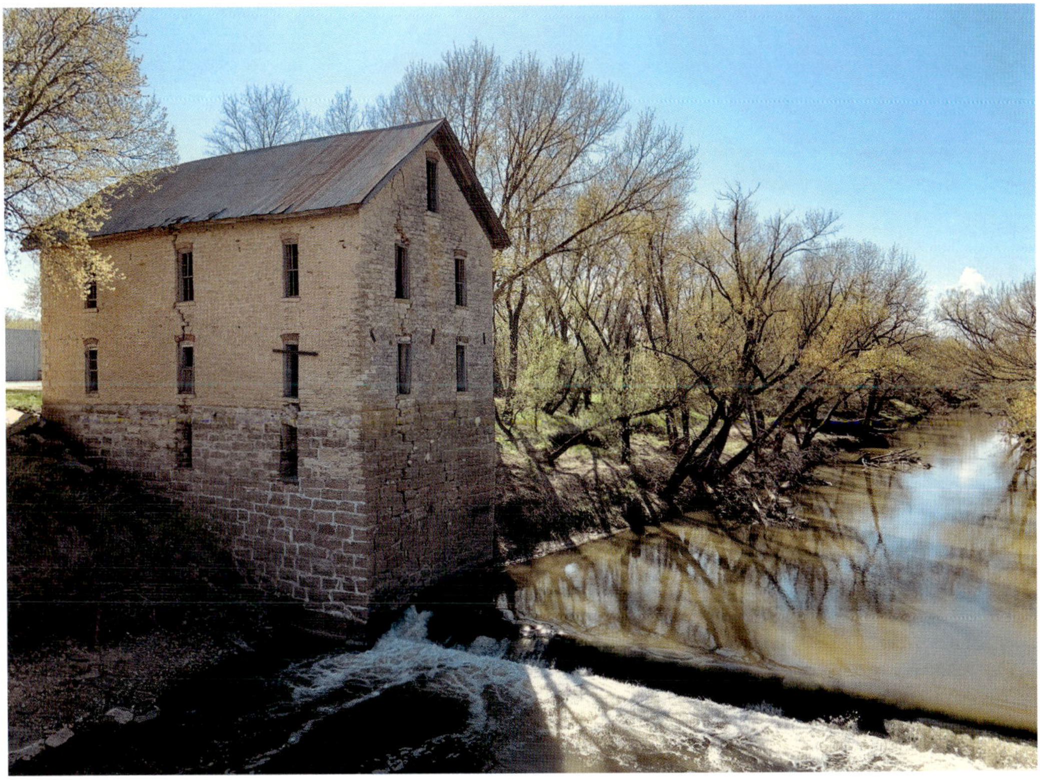

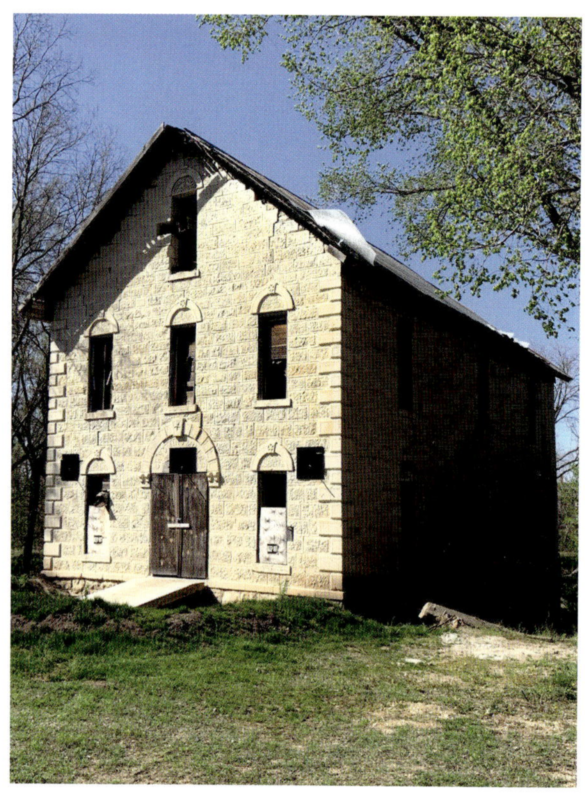

Front of the Drinkwater and Schriver Mill in Cedar Point, April 2020.

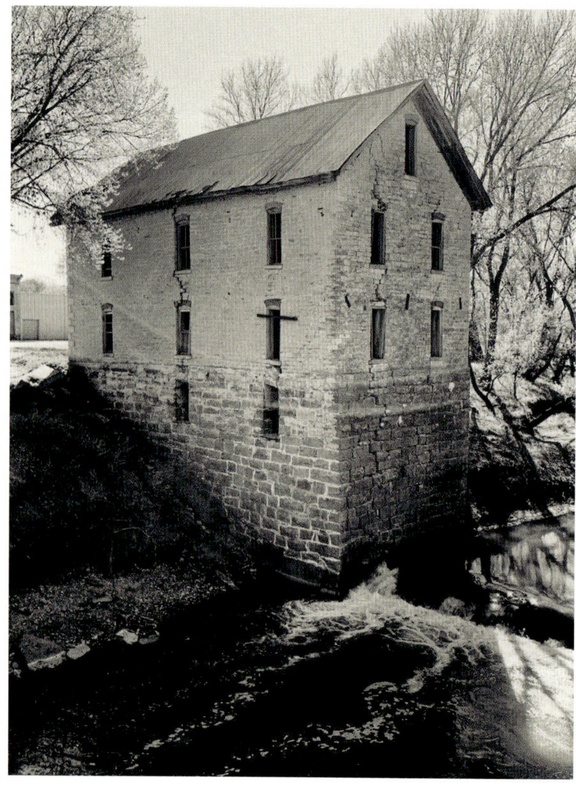

Visible cracks cover the side and back of the Drinkwater and Schriver Mill in Cedar Point, April 2020.

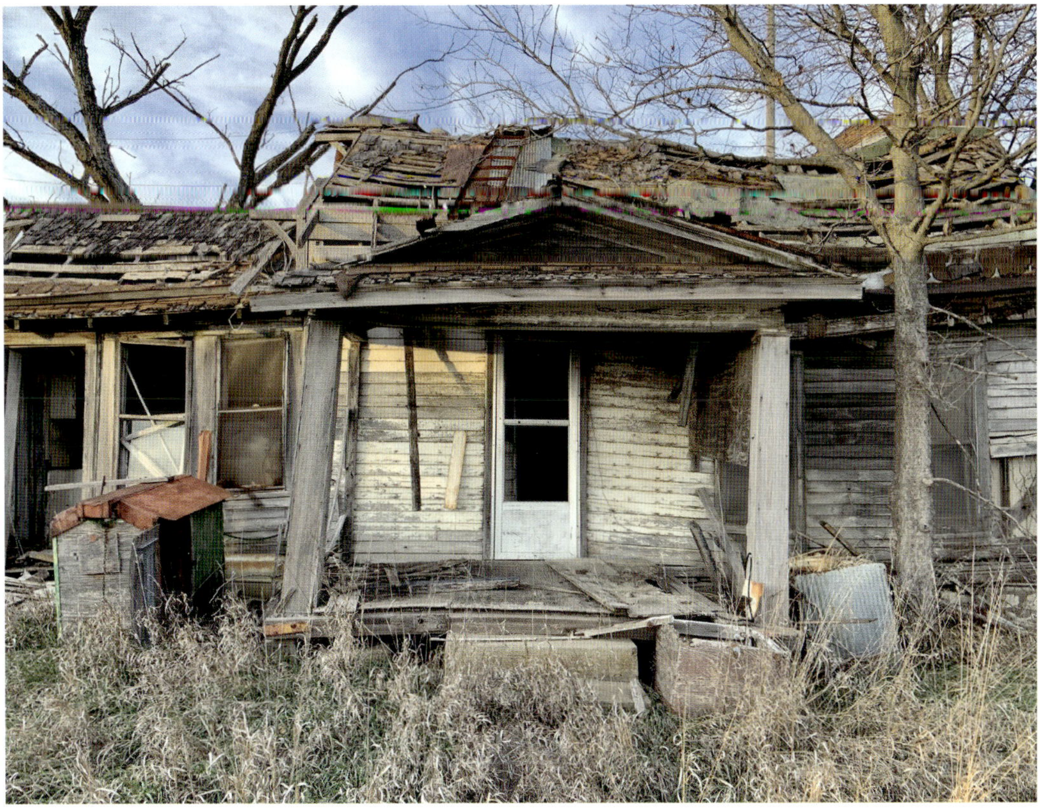

Above: Abandoned house in Lyndon, November 2020.

Right: Built in 1882, this church would later become a post office for the town of Skiddy, seen in November 2020.

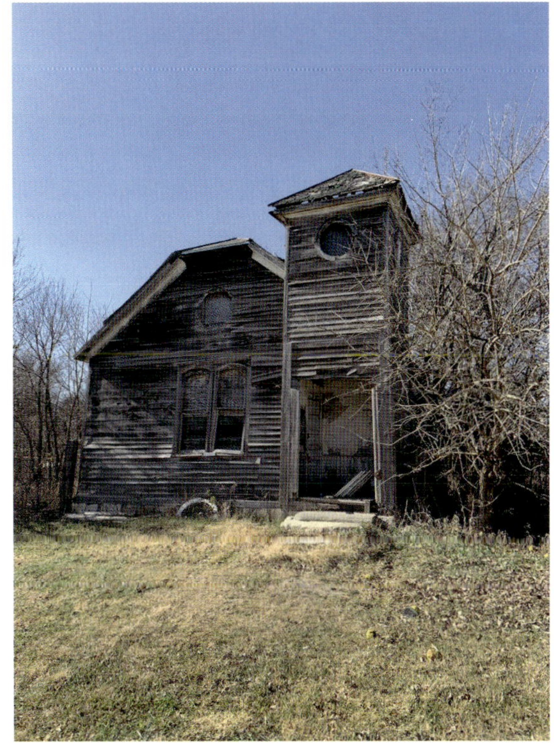

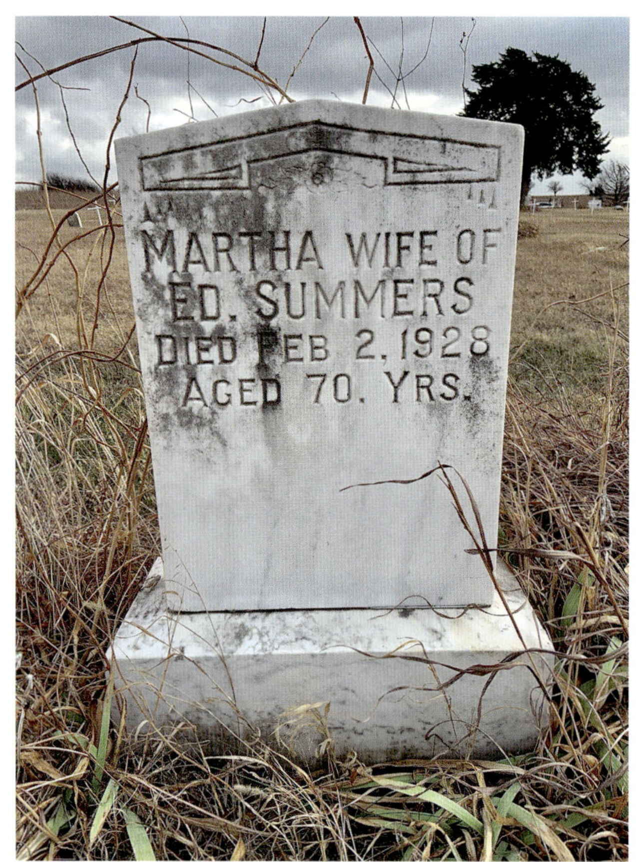

Left: Headstone for Martha Summers, November 2020. Born in 1858, she was the wife of Ed Summers. She is buried next to Ed in the Dunlap Colored Cemetery in Dunlap.

Below: Headstone for Ed Summers, November 2020. Born in 1851. After his wife, Martha, passed away in 1928, Ed would go on to live another twenty-three years without her. He would pass away at the age of 100 and is buried next to Martha in the Dunlap Colored Cemetery in Dunlap.

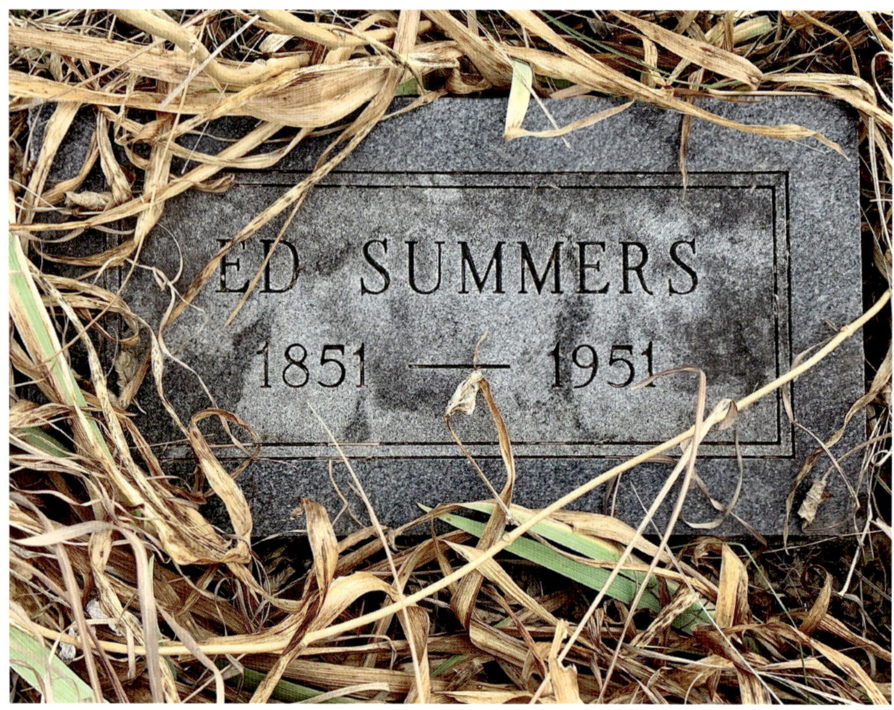

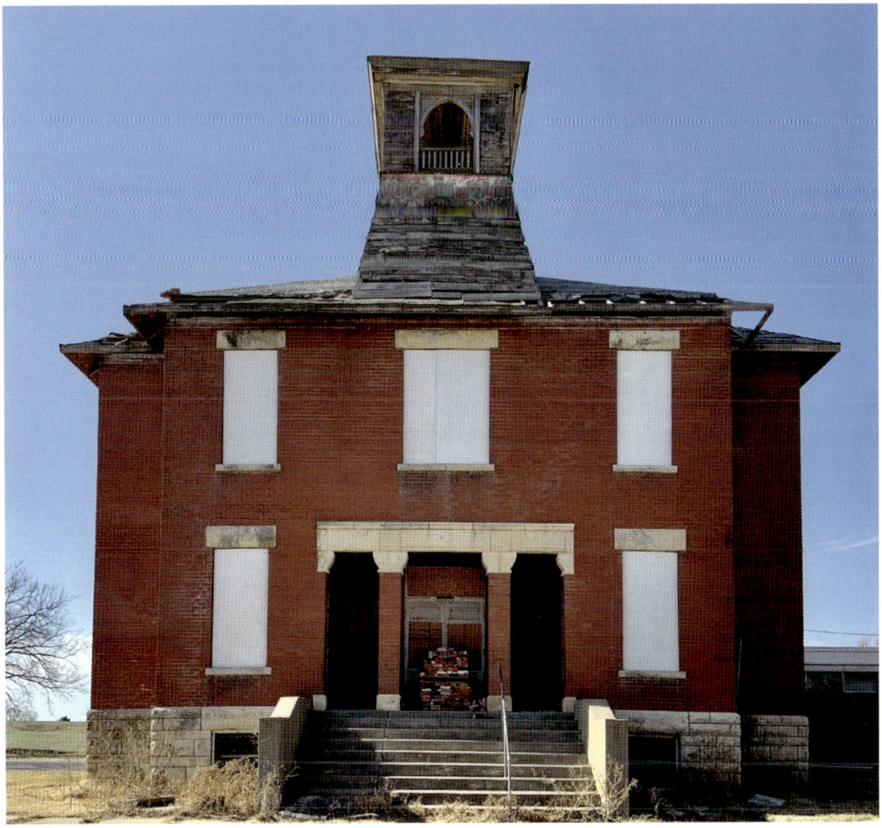

Above: Abandoned school in Woodbine, November 2020.

Right: Old TV on the ground inside an abandoned and collapsing garage in Elmo, November 2020.

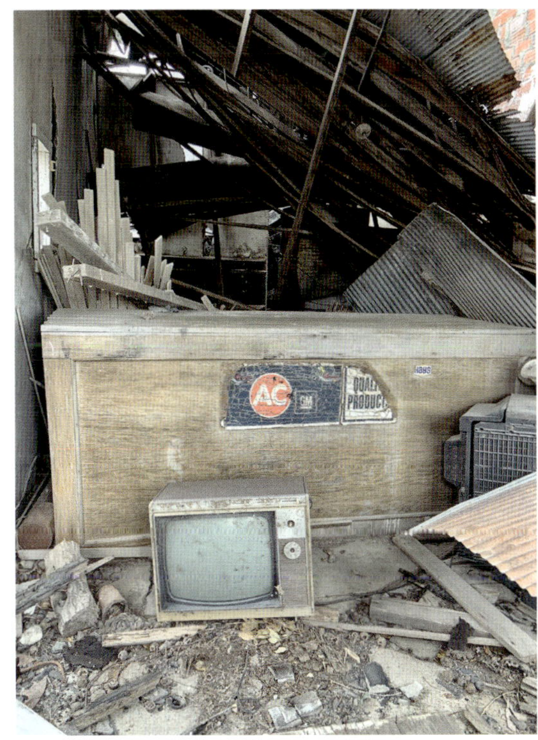

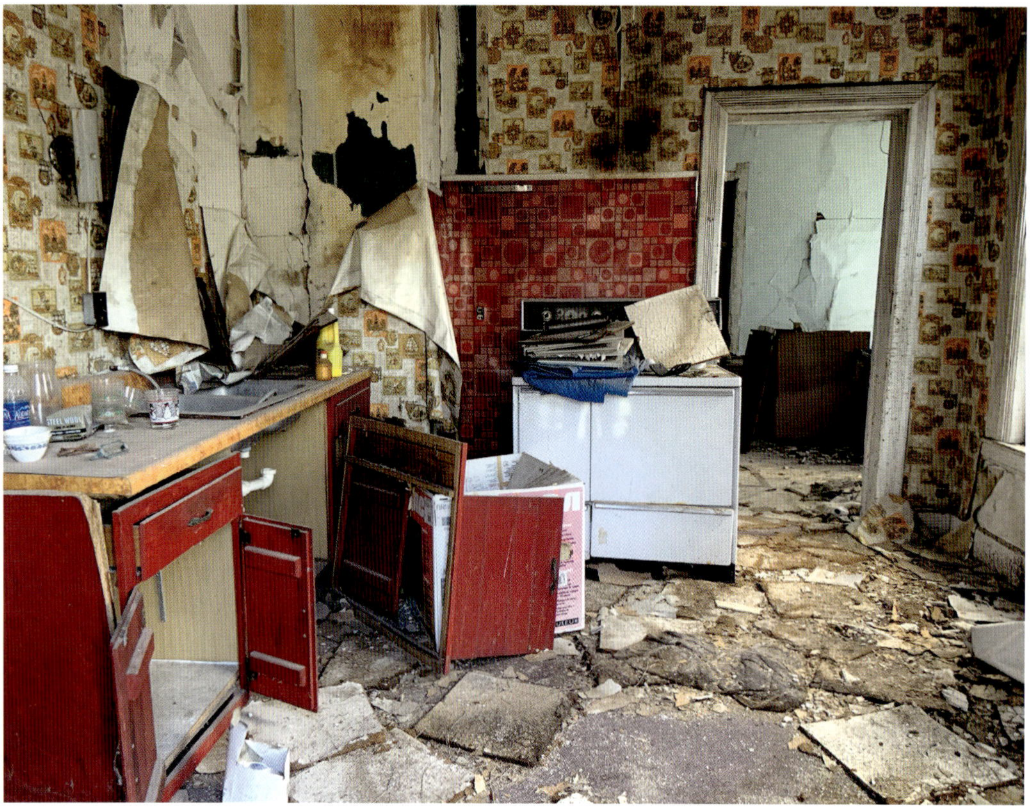

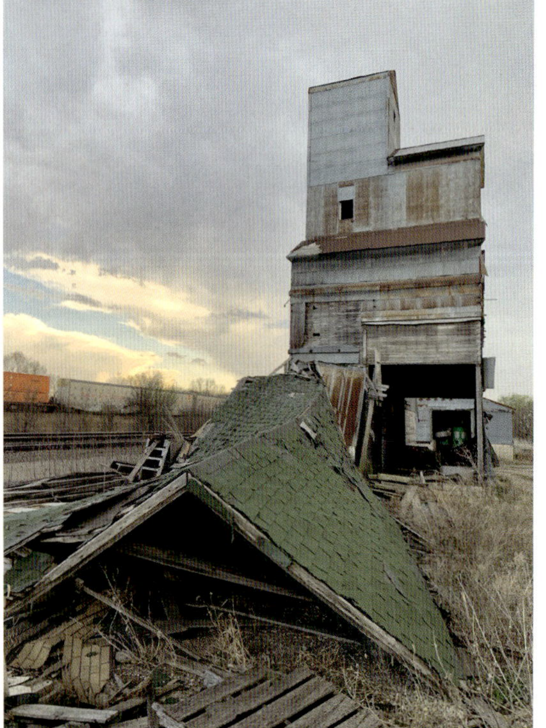

Above: Kitchen inside an abandoned house in Elmdale, April 2020.

Left: An abandoned and collapsing grain elevator a few miles outside Strong City, April 2020.

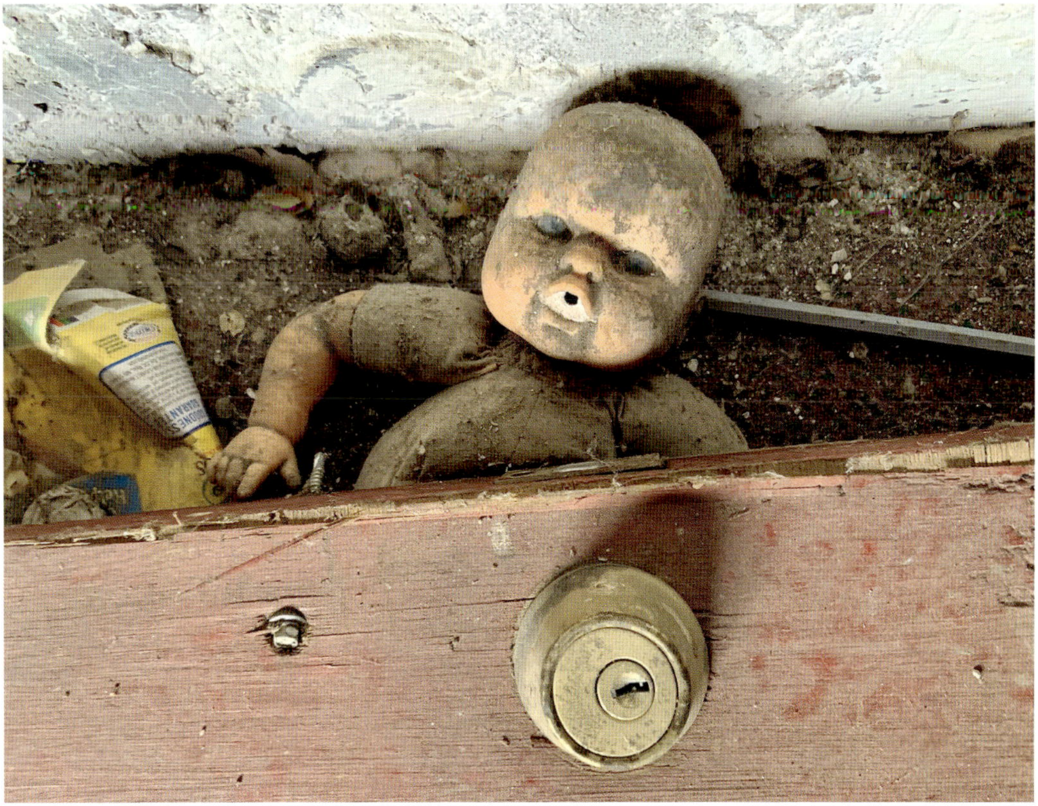

Above: A forgotten baby doll found in an abandoned house in Dunlap, November 2020.

Right: An abandoned treehouse in Woodbine, November 2020.

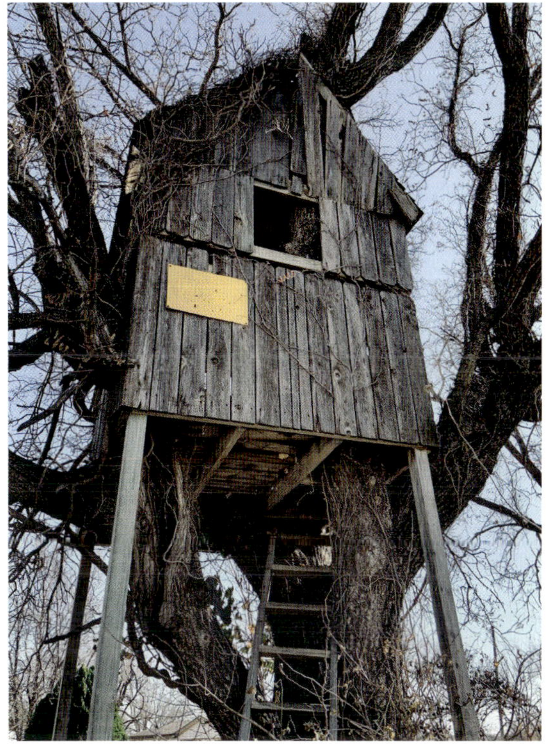

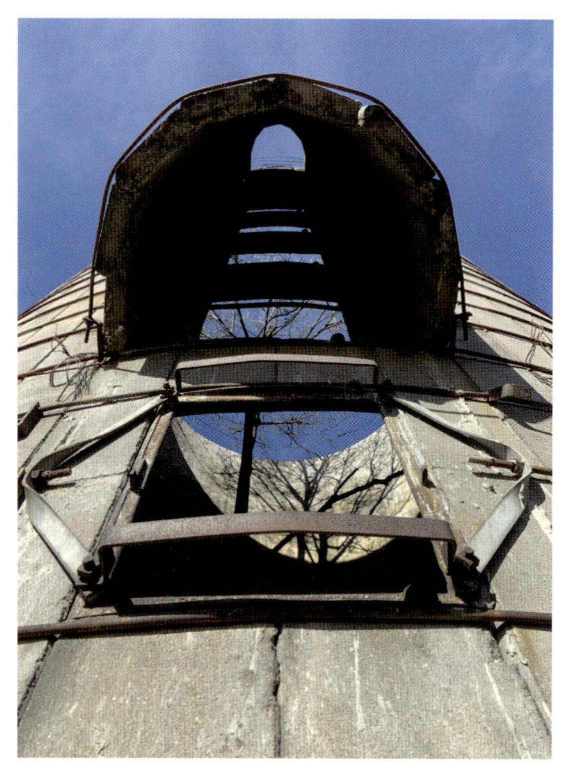

Left: A tree growing inside an abandoned silo in Wellsville, November 2020.

Below: Kitten wallpaper in an abandoned house outside Paola, November 2020.

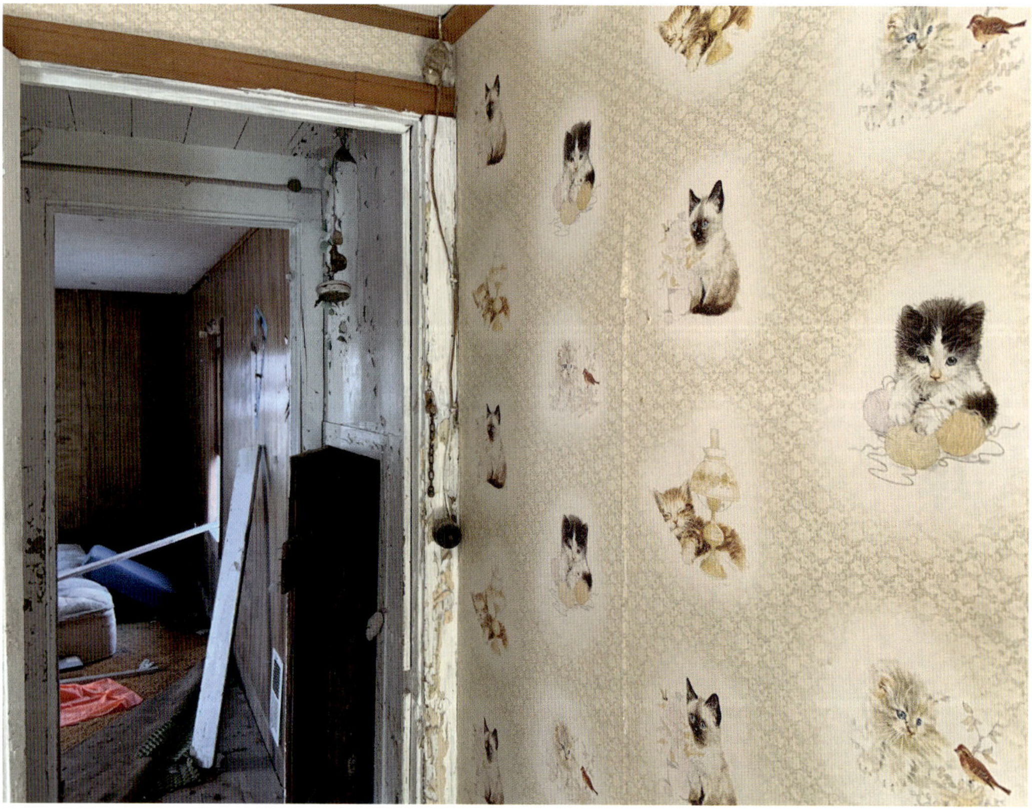

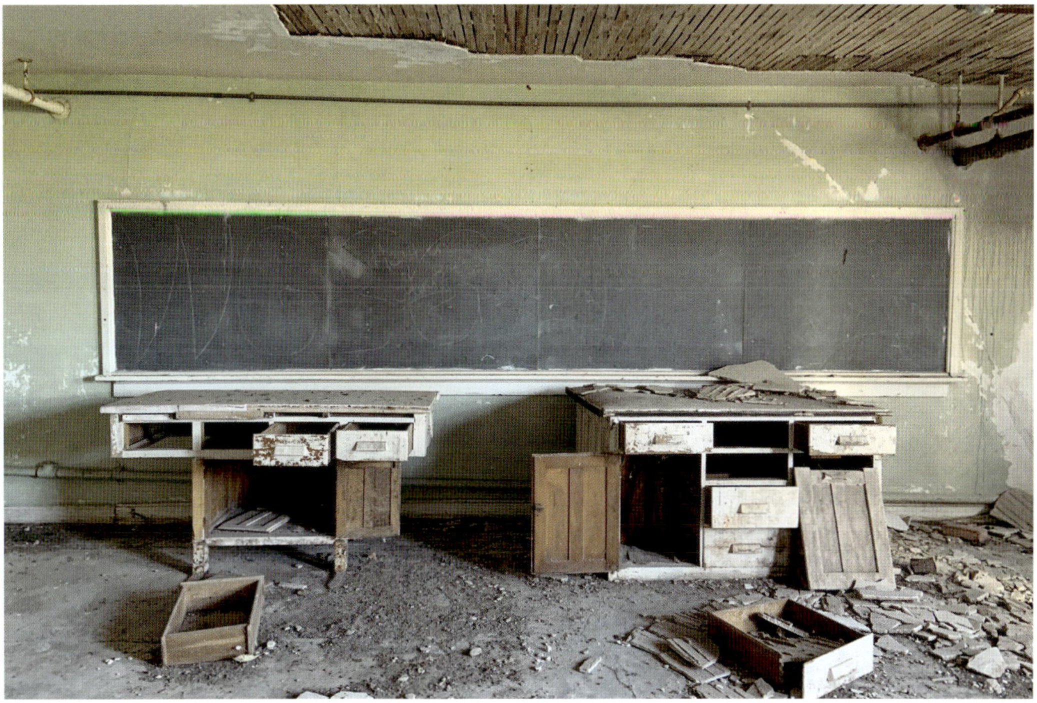

Desks left behind in this abandoned school in Woodbine, November 2020.

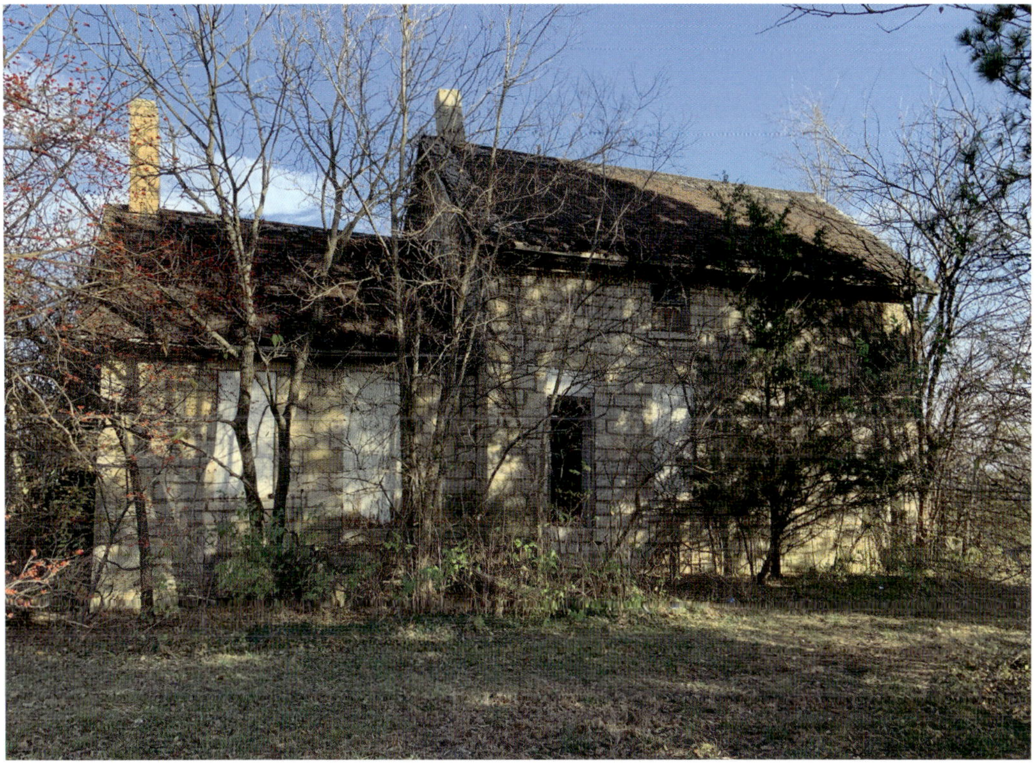

An abandoned house covered in trees and vines outside Ottawa, November 2020.

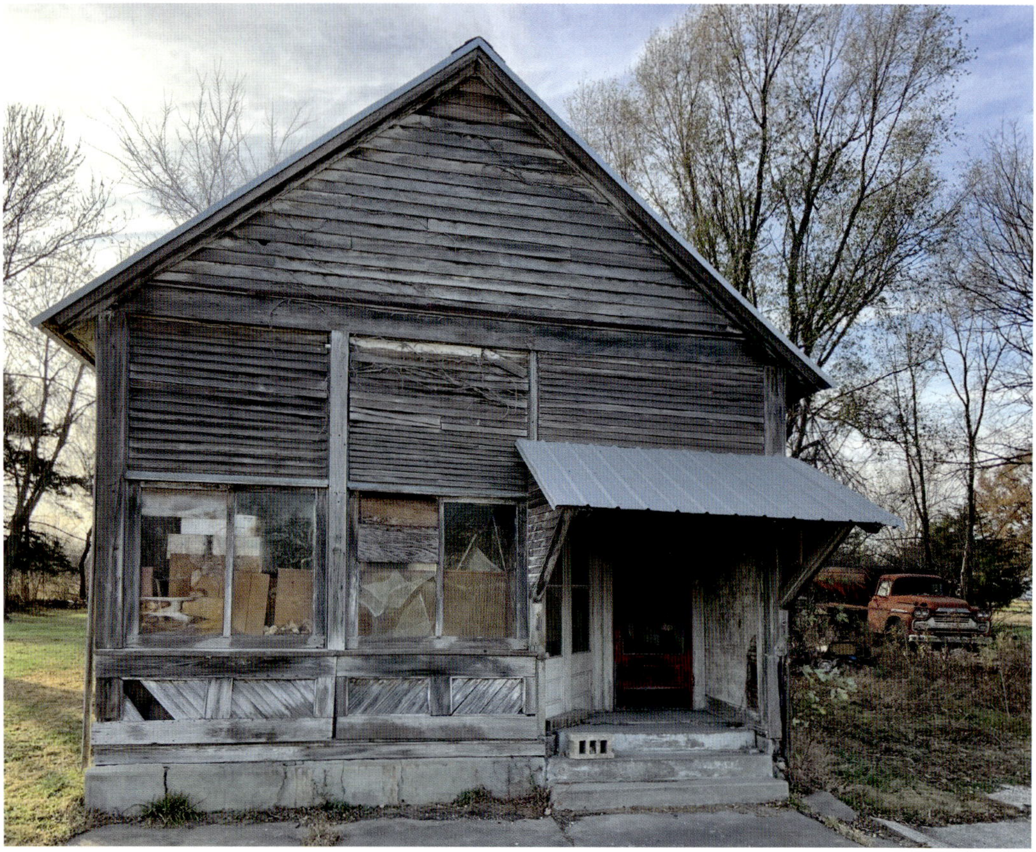

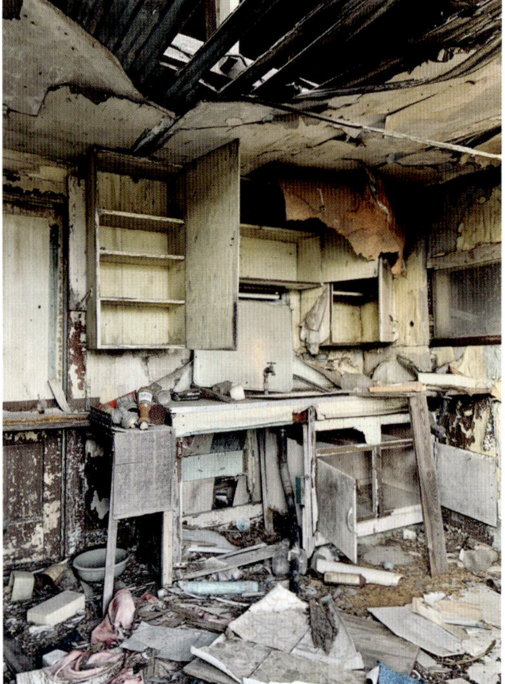

Above: An abandoned building and truck in Williamsburg, November 2020.

Left: Collapsing kitchen in an abandoned house in Lyndon, November 2020.

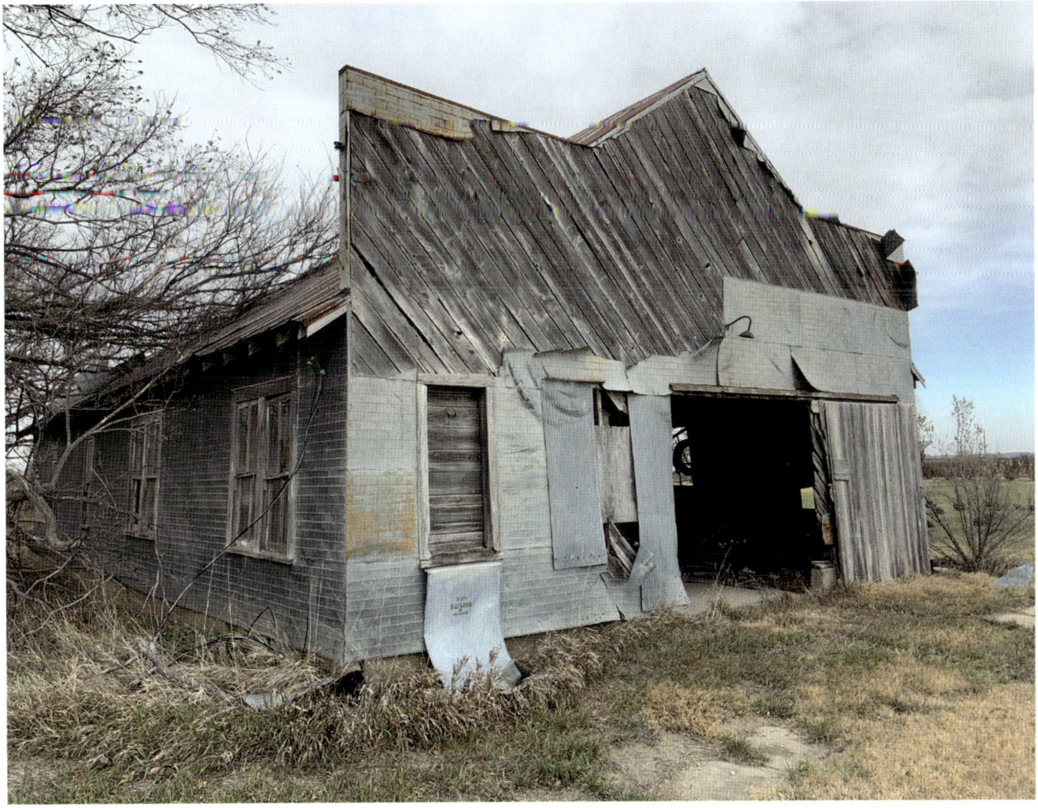

An abandoned building in Elmo, November 2020.

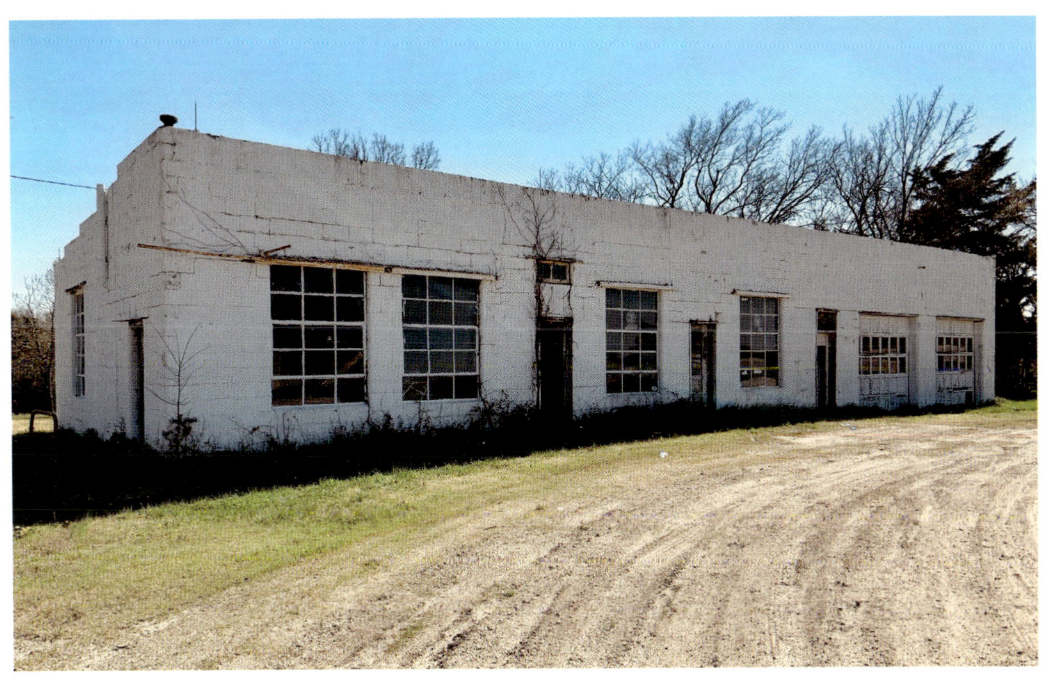

An abandoned service station outside Florence, April 2020.

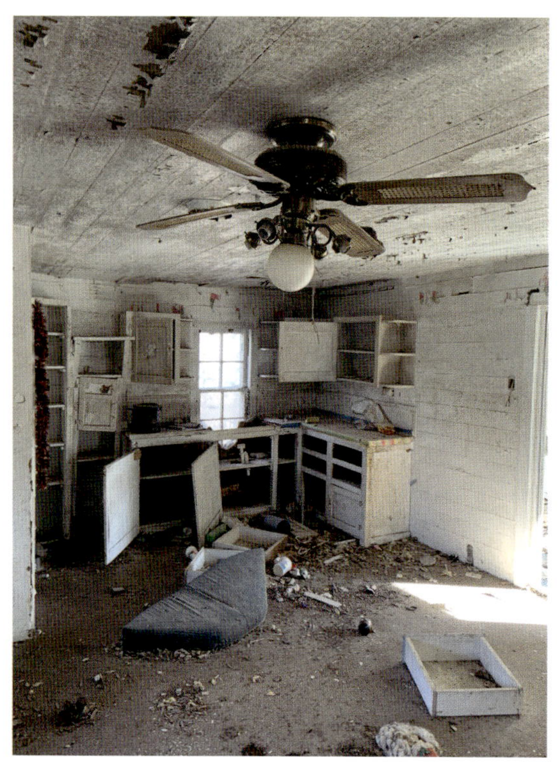

Left: Kitchen in an abandoned house in Paola, November 2020.

Below: Inside an abandoned house outside Ottawa, November 2020.

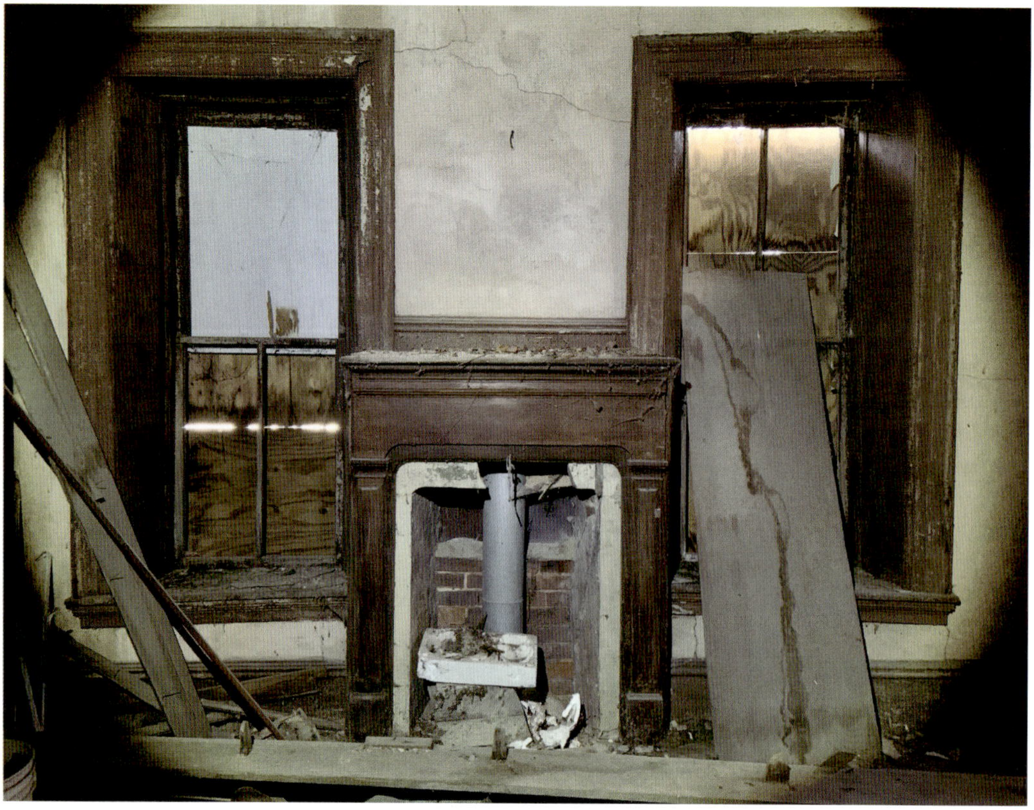

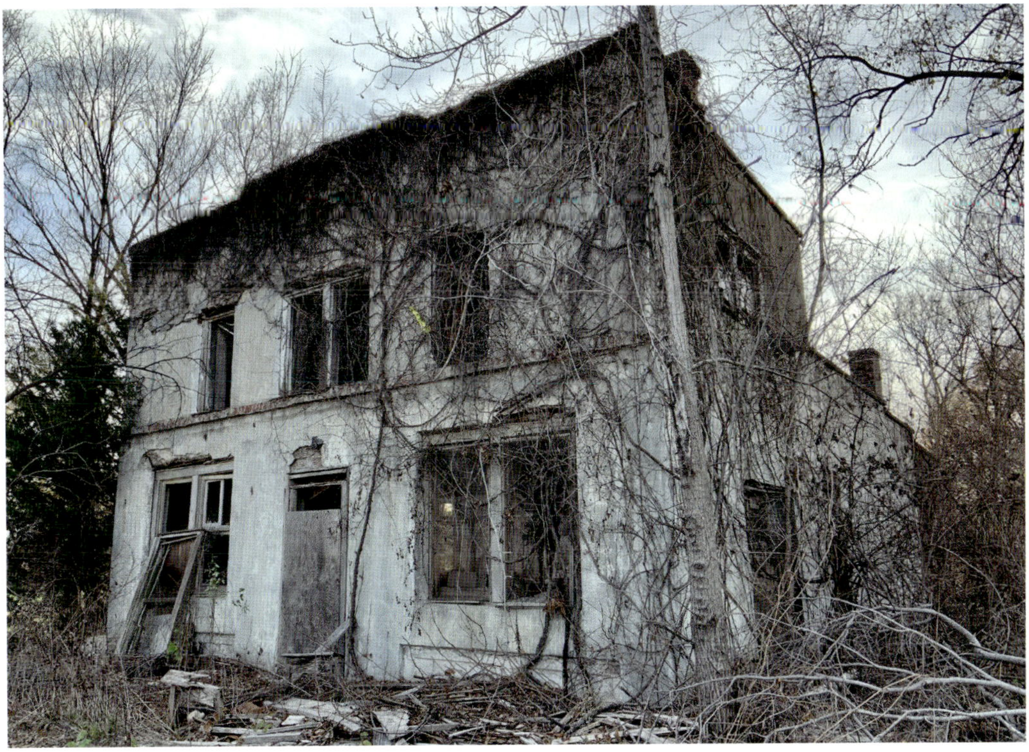

Above: An abandoned building in Williamsburg, November 2020.

Right: Side entrance to an abandoned school in Woodbine, November 2020.

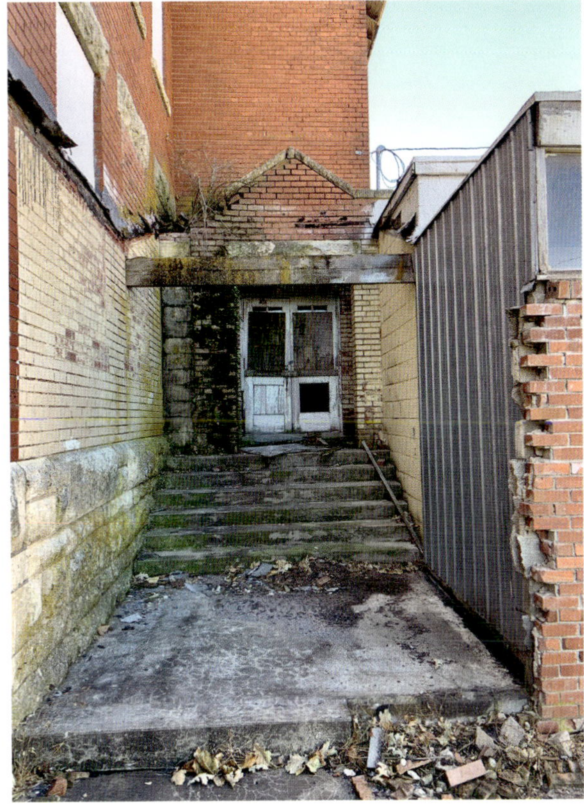

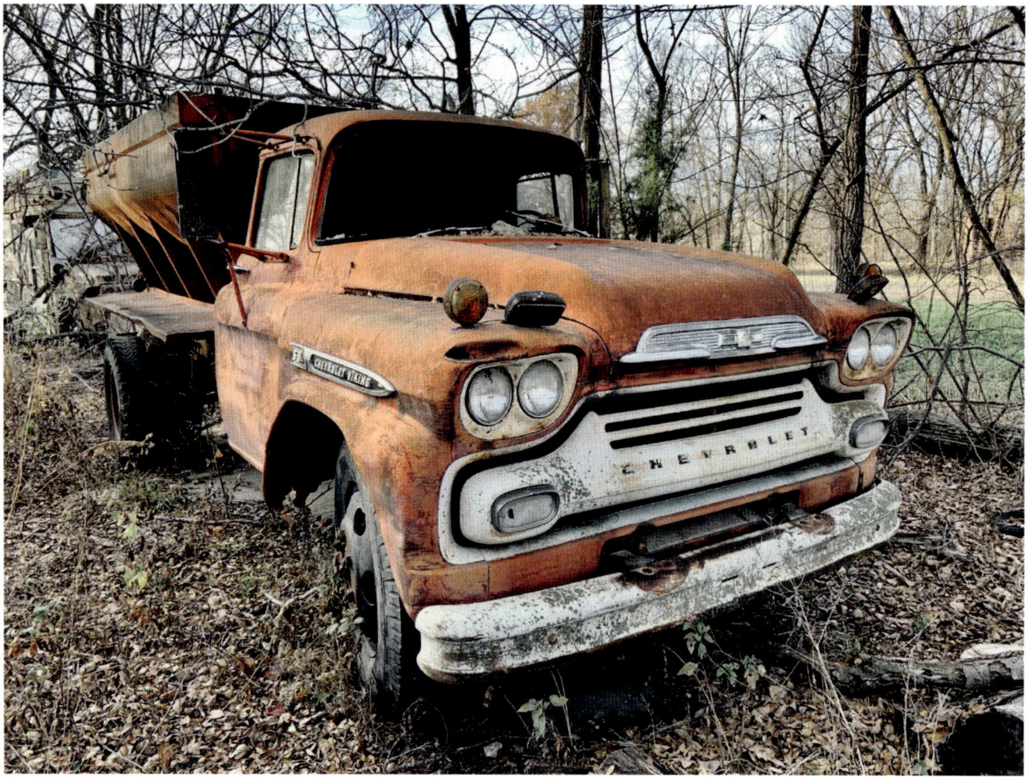

An abandoned truck in Williamsburg, November 2020.

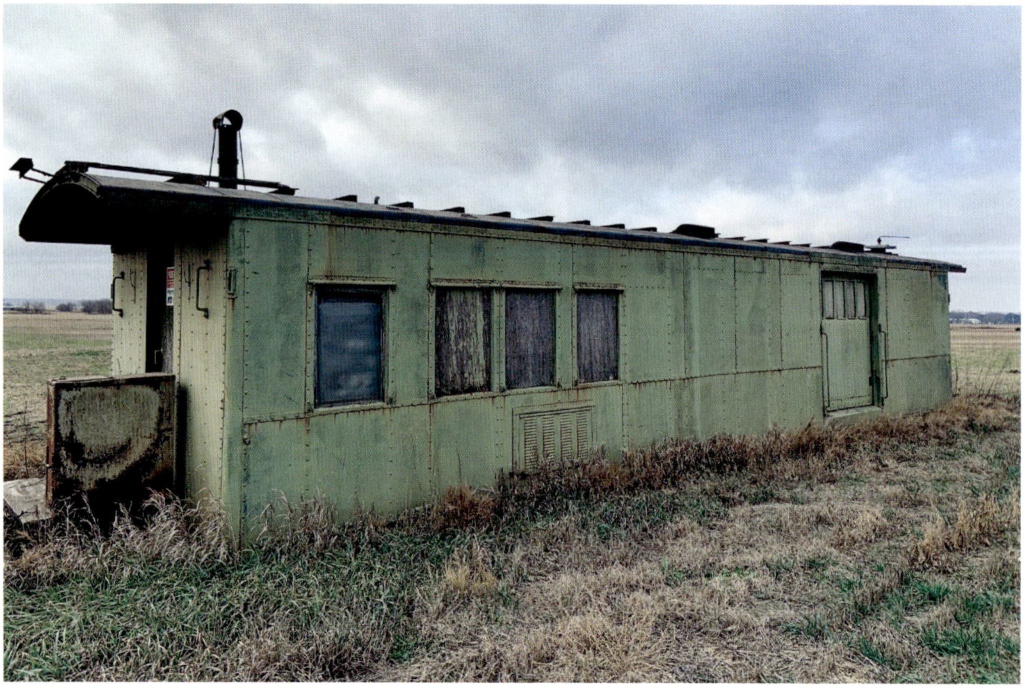

An abandoned train car in a field in Americus, November 2020.

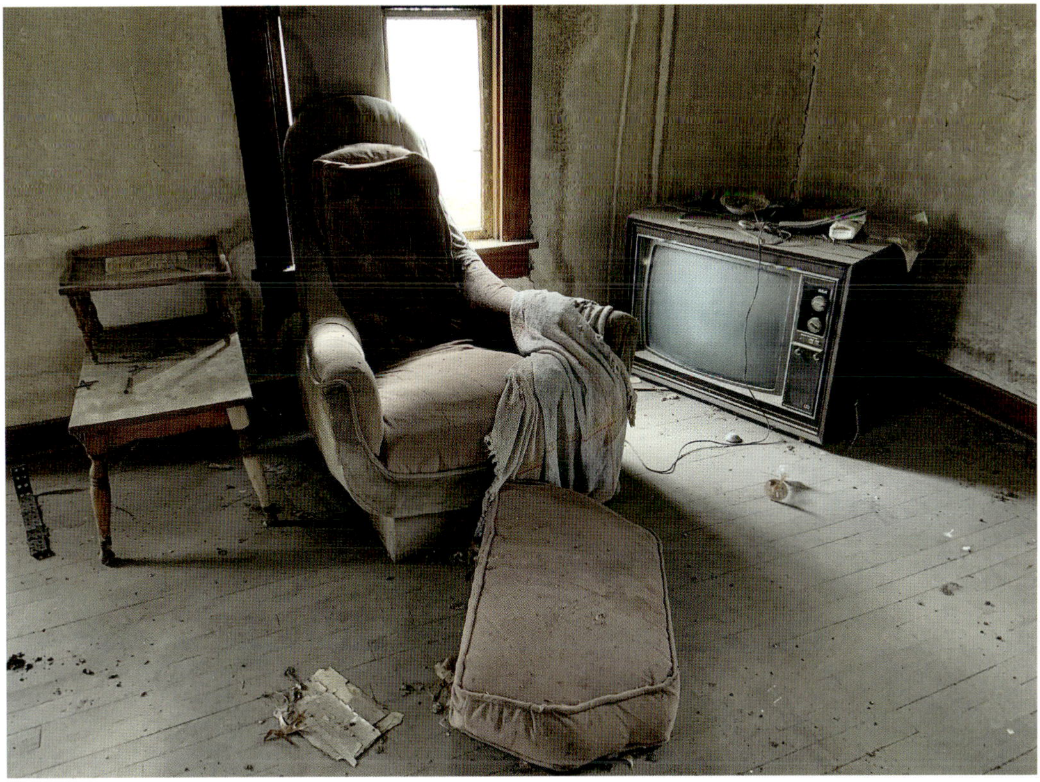

Forgotten furniture in an abandoned house in Dunlap, November 2020.

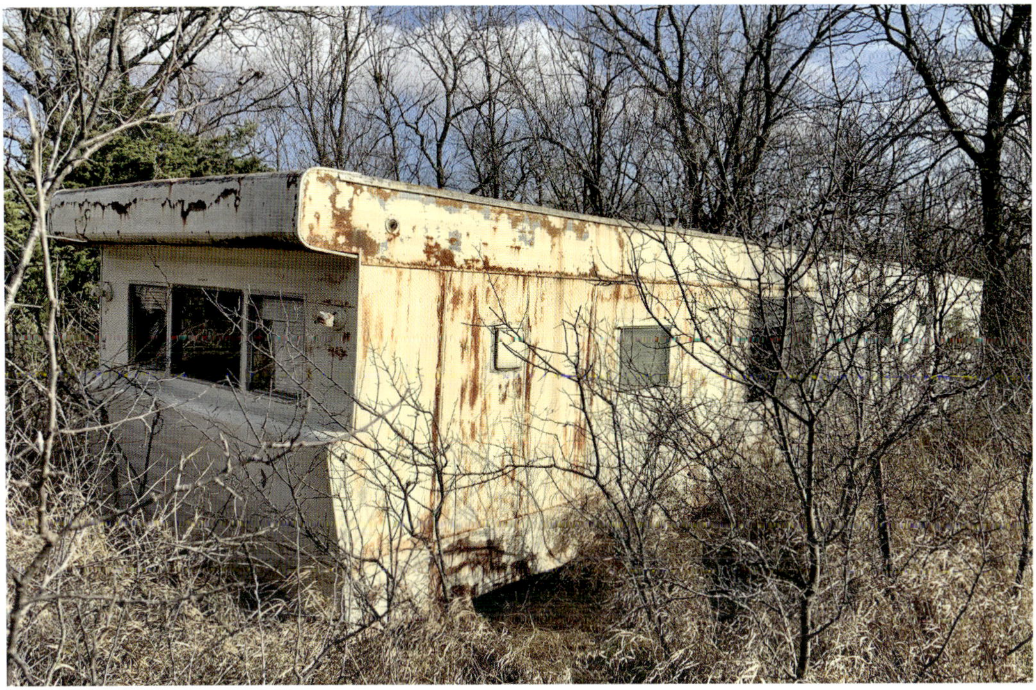

An abandoned trailer in Bushong, November 2020.

5

CORONADO HEIGHTS

Another notable building, a little farther into Eastern Kansas, located just outside the Swedish town of Lindsborg, is Coronado Heights. Not abandoned today, the popular stone castle tells a story of the abandoned expedition for the Seven Cities of Gold. It was named after Francisco Vasquez de Coronado, a Spanish conquistador from the 1540s. It is widely believed among historians that Francisco traveled from Mexico through the area we now know as Kansas, looking for the legendary Seven Cities of Gold. The first leg of the expedition in 1540 led him to the New Mexico/Arizona area, where he was unsuccessful in finding any gold or treasure.

He was then told the story about wealth possessed by the Quivira nation of the Great Plains area. A year later, Francisco led another expedition to locate the riches supposedly located in central Kansas. Once he arrived in the area, he stayed for almost a month and was again unsuccessful in his search for gold and wealth. He abandoned his futile search for the Seven Cities of Gold and returned to New Mexico to meet up with his army in 1542. Upon his return to Mexico City later that same year, he would face legal and financial troubles stemming from his failed expeditions. Four years later, Francisco would be cleared of the charges against him and he would remain in Mexico City until his death in 1554.

The Seven Cities of Gold is just a legend. However, in 1915, a piece of chainmail was found in the area by a local teacher. That discovery would give the legend the possibility of being more than just a legend. Later, in 1919, the area was purchased by the Smoky Valley Historical Society for the development of Coronado Heights, but due to the stock market and the Great Depression, the project, including the sandstone castle monument, was not completed until 1936.

Today, Coronado Heights covers 16 acres, and the castle sits hundreds of feet overlooking the Smoky Hill River valley. The castle is a popular destination for the area. Many visitors walk or bike the trails up to the scenic overlook; however, driving straight to the top is also an option. The castle offers an amazing view where you can see for miles all around.

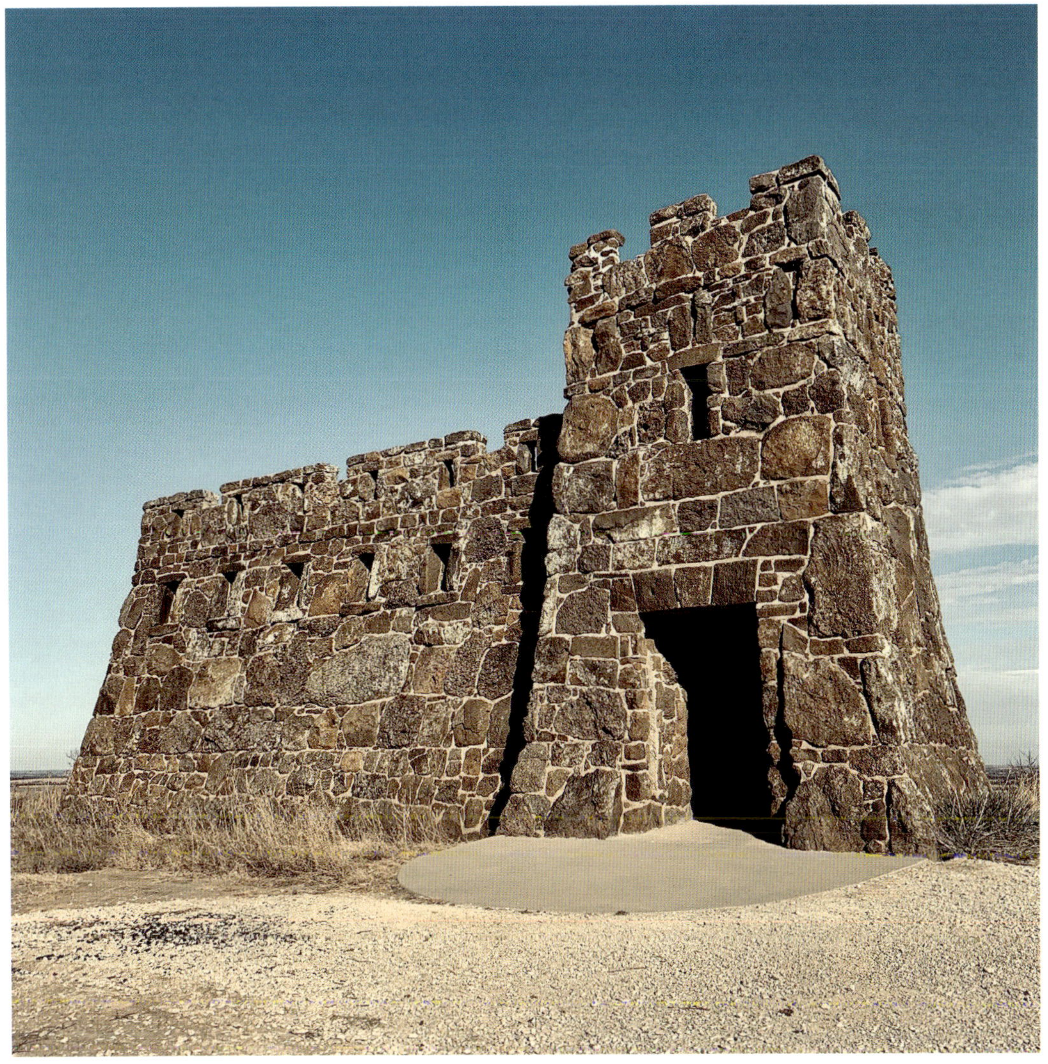

The stone castle at Coronado Heights outside Lindsborg, November 2020.

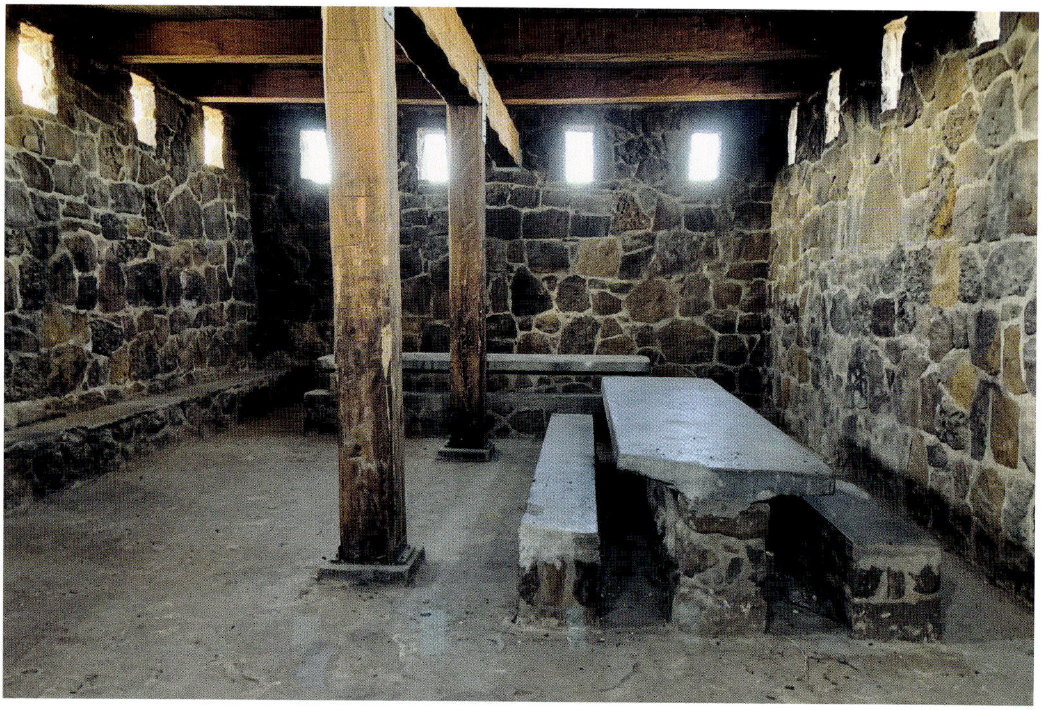

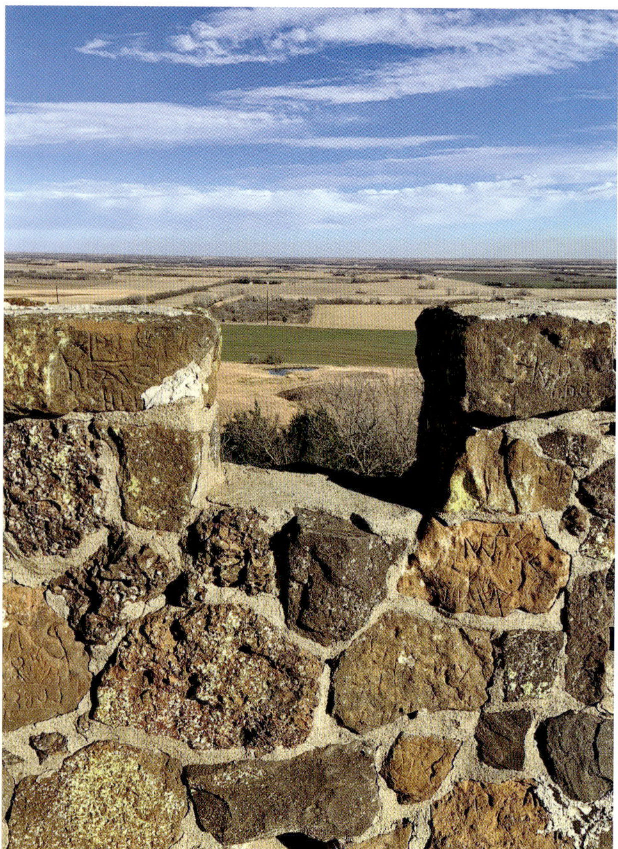

Above: Inside the castle at Coronado Heights outside Lindsborg, November 2020.

Left: Looking east from the top of the castle at Coronado Heights, outside Lindsborg, November 2020.

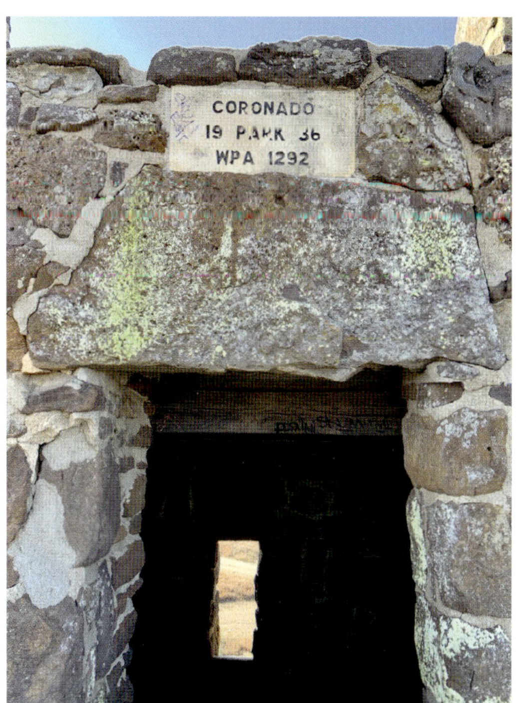

Right: The 1936 plaque for the Works Progress Administration (W.P.A.), which built the castle at Coronado Heights, located outside Lindsborg, seen in November 2020.

Below: Top of the castle at Coronado Heights, outside Lindsborg, November 2020.

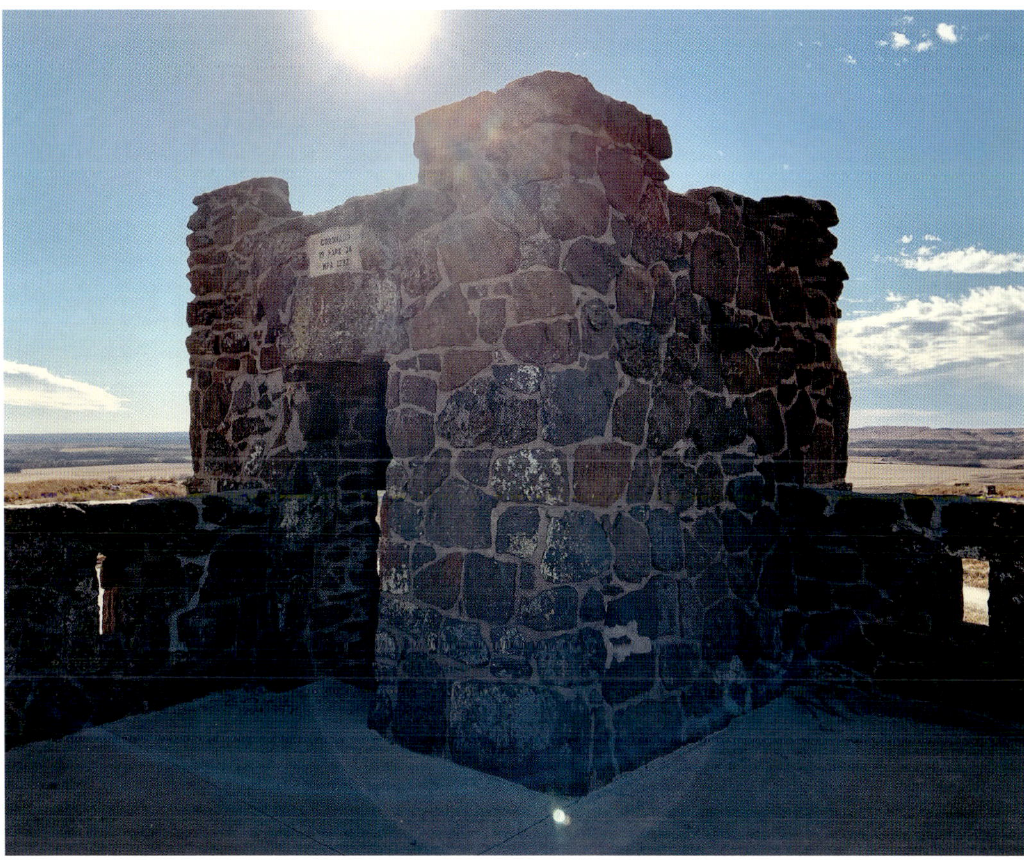

6

ONE-ROOM SCHOOLHOUSES

This next chapter is not about a place in particular but more about the many one-room schoolhouses throughout Kansas. At one time, the number of these schoolhouses was as high as 9,000 statewide. Each schoolhouse differed by design, but all of their stories play out the same way—a story of early establishment, educational supply and demand, and the evolution of that demand becoming the demise of the one-room schoolhouse.

A year after Kansas became the thirty-fourth state, President Lincoln signed the Homestead Act of 1862, giving "citizens or future citizens up to 160 acres of public land provided they live on it, improve it, and pay a small registration fee." That act set the wheels in motion. With early settlers and farmers came town establishment, and schools and businesses were built to meet the needs of those settlers and farmers. Each schoolhouse was its own district and educated on average about twenty to forty students covering all eight grades. Over the years, the number of farming communities would decrease and larger schools would be built to accommodate many schools becoming consolidated. Thousands of these schoolhouses would close throughout the 1940s, until 1963, when it was recorded that only 427 were still in use at the time. Today, the many remaining one-room schoolhouses are just roadside reminders of the days of early education.

These are the stories of three of those remaining schoolhouses. I was unable to locate any detailed information online about these three schools. I then contacted county historians. The historical societies of Geary, Lyon, and Osage County are a top-notch group of historians. They all do an amazing job at keeping history preserved for all of us.

District 88: Hobbston School

Located in Osage County, 3 miles outside of Osage City, is the former District 88 schoolhouse. According to historical documents, District 88 was also known as Hobbston School and was nicknamed "Hobbs School" for short. Hobbs was organized in 1868 and, like many schools of the state, educated around twenty students throughout all eight grades. Eventually, Osage City would build a bigger school to accommodate the growing town. Enrolment would decline down to just four to five students in its last year. The need for the small school had run its course and the remaining students would be transferred to the newer school in town. The schoolhouse was closed in 1958.

Today, the District 88 schoolhouse sits on a lonely corner, surrounded by farmland on the outskirts of town. The brick school has been well taken care of, at least from the outside. The woodwork was weathered, but you could still see a couple of the letters of District 88 painted above the door. The windows were all boarded up, so I was unable to see if there was still some desk and school stuff in there or if it was in bad condition. I always imagine it looking the way it did, the day it closed. Although I did not get to see inside, it was one of the better-maintained buildings.

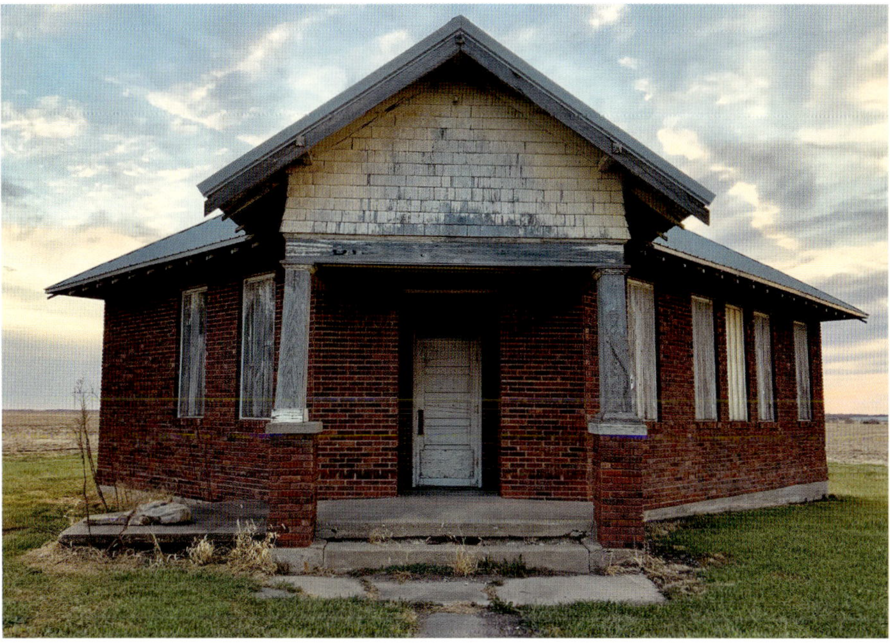

Front of the District 88 schoolhouse, November 2020. It was also known as Hobbston School. Located outside Osage City, the one-room schoolhouse closed in 1958.

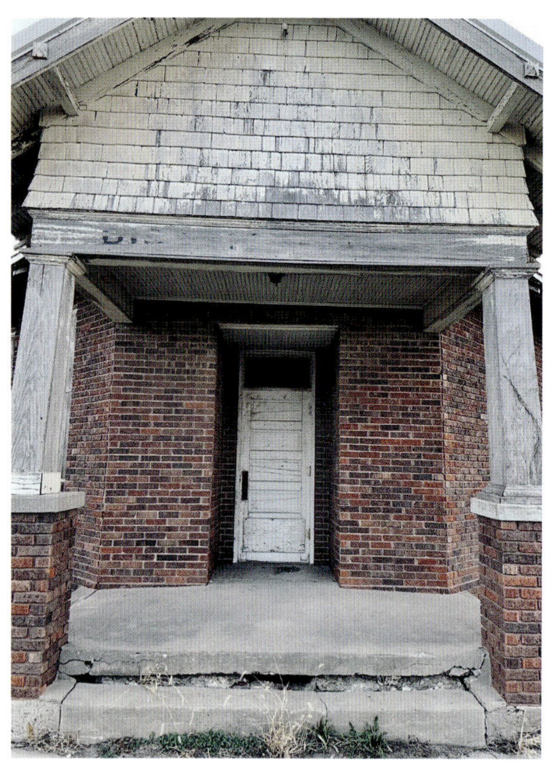

Left: You can still faintly see the "DIS" in District 88, painted over the porch on the Hobbston School located outside Osage City, November 2020.

Below: The Hobbston School sits on a lonely corner, surrounded by farmland outside Osage City, November 2020.

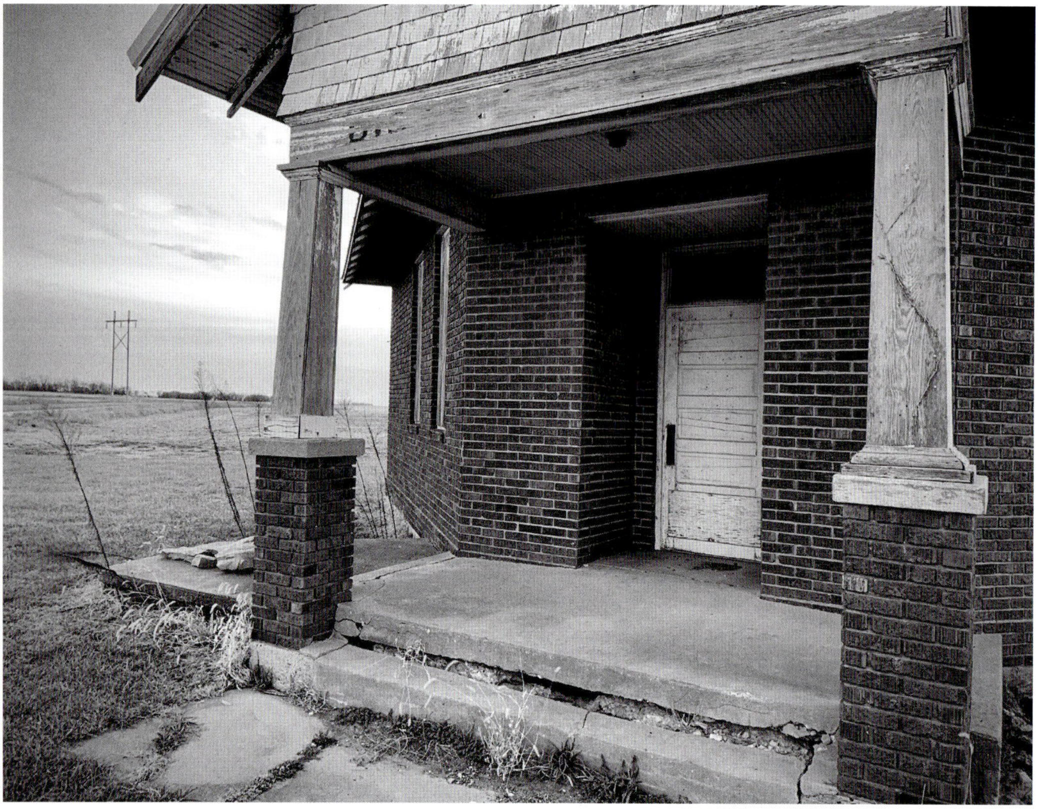

District 72: Butler School

In the next county over, between Americus and Dunlap, on a Lyon County back road, is the District 72 schoolhouse. Organized in 1874 and for the cost of $800, District 72 is also referred to as the Butler School, after John Butler, an early settler that campaigned for the school to be built and went on to be on the first school board. The story of District 72 plays out like all the other small schools throughout Kansas. However, with District 72, we gain more insight into early Kansas education with the added detail of the school rating system. I was made aware of the early school ratings from the "Class B Elementary School" rating plate still attached to the front porch awning. It was a point system devised by the state of Kansas, to determine if a school was Class "A," "B," or "C." How many points a school received was based on many factors, such as school equipment and supplies, the teacher and their teaching experience, the condition and size of the school, and how many books were in the library, to name a few. The more a school had, the better the class rating. District 72 was a Class "B." Out of the possible 1,000 points, District 72 had 850 to 950 points. Knowing the rating for a Class "B," that does not leave as wide a margin for Class "A" ratings. At the height of student enrollment, District 72 reached around twenty and also taught all eight grades. Over the remaining years, enrollment would continue to decrease until 1955–1956, the school's final year, when only four students attended District 72.

Similar to District 88, this schoolhouse also sits on a corner between towns. There are still original additions to the school property. The double-seater outhouse sits out back behind the school and the metal water hand pump was still out front. Peeking through the windows, I could see rows of desks, not original but definitely old school. The paint on the design textured ceiling and walls was now peeling and you can see the darker wall behind peeking through the spots where the paint had fallen off. Even though this was all observed through a window, I felt as if I was looking into the windows of an early education time capsule, frozen in 1956 when District 72 closed its doors for the last time as a school.

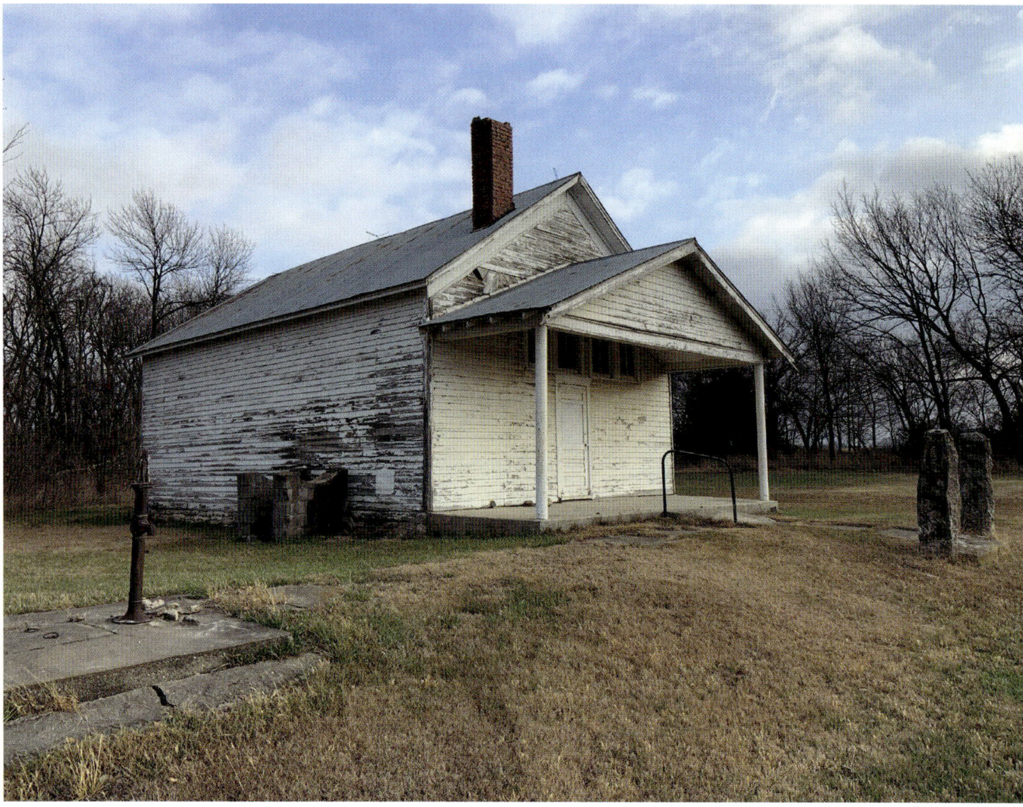

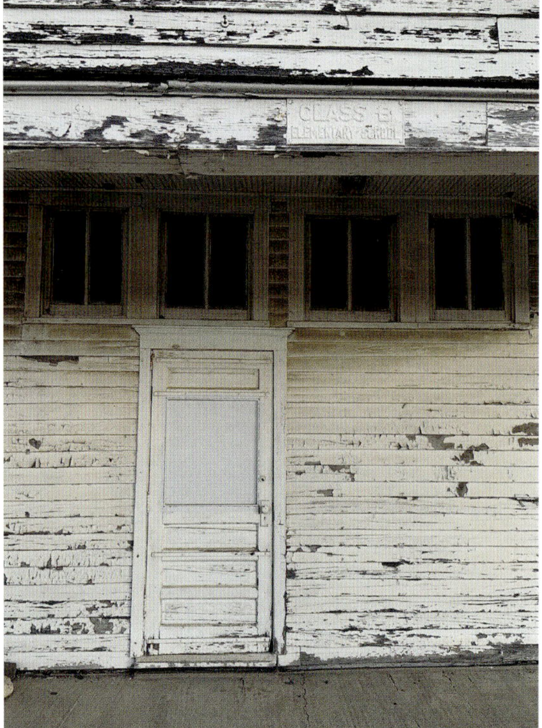

Above: Front of the District 72 schoolhouse, November 2020. Located outside Americus, the one-room schoolhouse closed in 1956.

Left: The "Class B" school rating sign still hangs on the front porch at the Butler School outside Americus, November 2020.

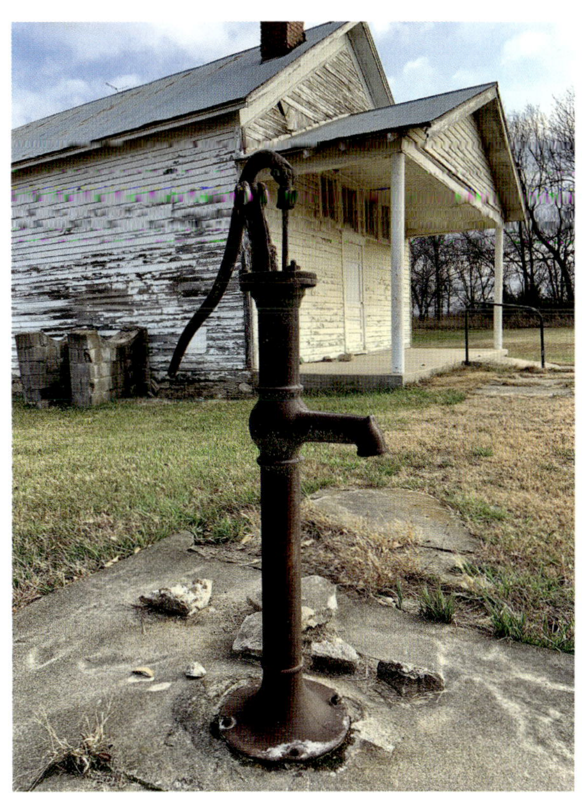

The hand-crank water pump outside the Butler School, just a few miles from Americus, November 2020.

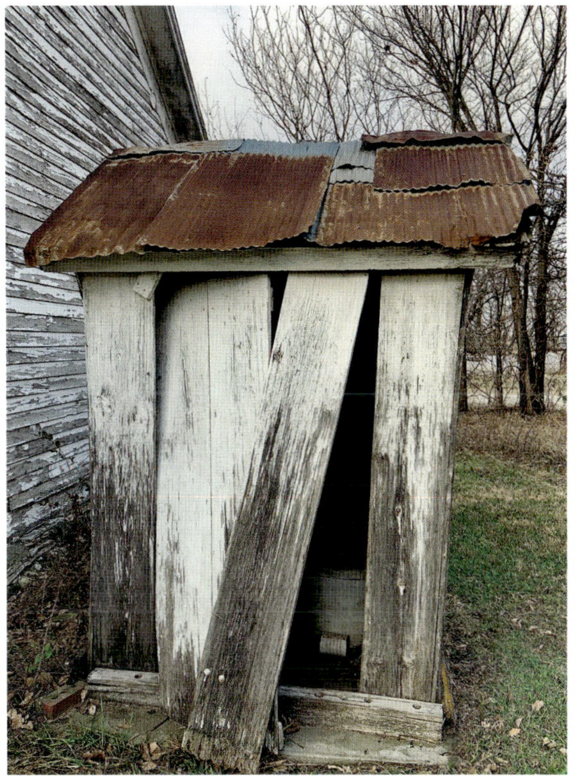

The double-seater outhouse behind the Butler School, located a few miles from Americus, November 2020.

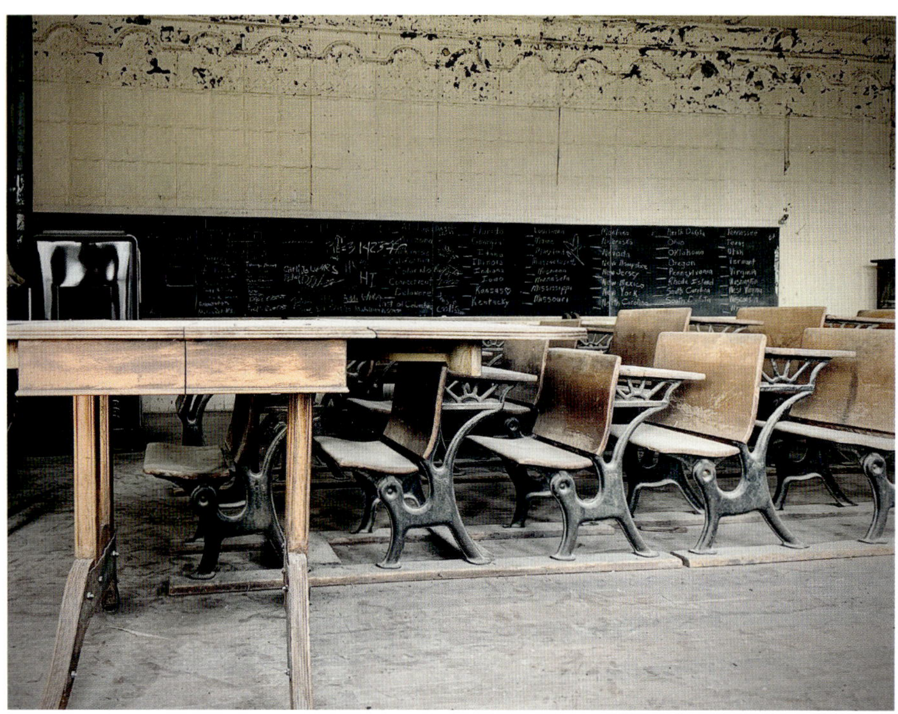

Peeking through the window, you get a view of old desks in orderly rows and the peeling paint from the textured designed walls inside the Butler School, located a few miles outside of Americus, November 2020.

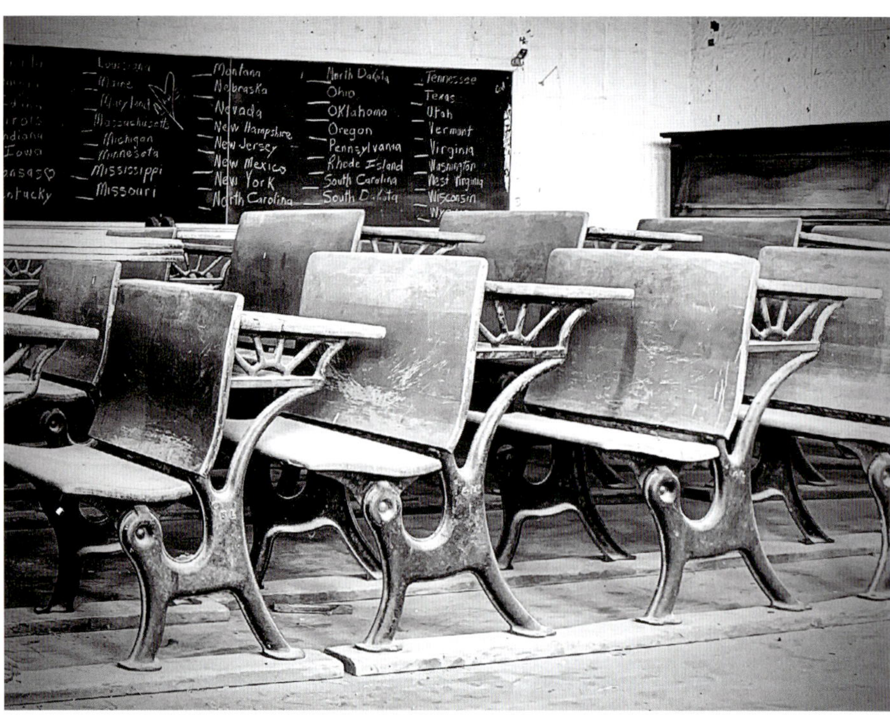

Close up of the student's desks inside the Butler School, located a few miles outside of Americus, November 2020.

District 12: Half Acre School

A couple of counties over, down multiple dirt roads, and in the middle of nowhere, is the District 12 schoolhouse. Established in 1865, District 12 was also called the Half Acre School. When first established, the school was to educate the children from Morris and Davis counties, but county unions were dissolved and boundary lines changed in the summer of 1872. With those changes, Morris County moved to another district, and District 12 was now educating both Davis and Geary County children. Over the years, District 12 would teach all eight grades and attendance ranged from fifty students on their best year, down to two students. When looking through the yearly school records, District 12 started seeing enrollment issues causing temporary closures throughout the 1940s. The school managed to get the number of students up for a few more years but would close again in 1956. District 12 would finally disorganize in 1959.

Finding the District 12 schoolhouse was mere happenstance. I was in the area to see a church that was also a post office in a town that was not much more than an intersection. We took the turn down another gravel road that led deeper into the vast openness of Eastern Kansas. Tucked back and slightly camouflaged by the trees was the small stone schoolhouse. The stone structure, itself, was still intact; however, the woodwork in and around it was very old and falling apart. It would not surprise me if that was the original wood from when the school was built. Besides a small front entryway, it was the traditional one big room for all the grades. I did like how the corner shelving was still there and was even though in bad shape, it was still recognizable. Unlike the previous schools, the District 12 schoolhouse has not been maintained and has weathered a lot of damages over the years. Looking at the surrounding trees and the thin veil of privacy they provide for the school, it was easy to see how in full summer bloom that the school would be almost completely hidden—like a secret in the trees.

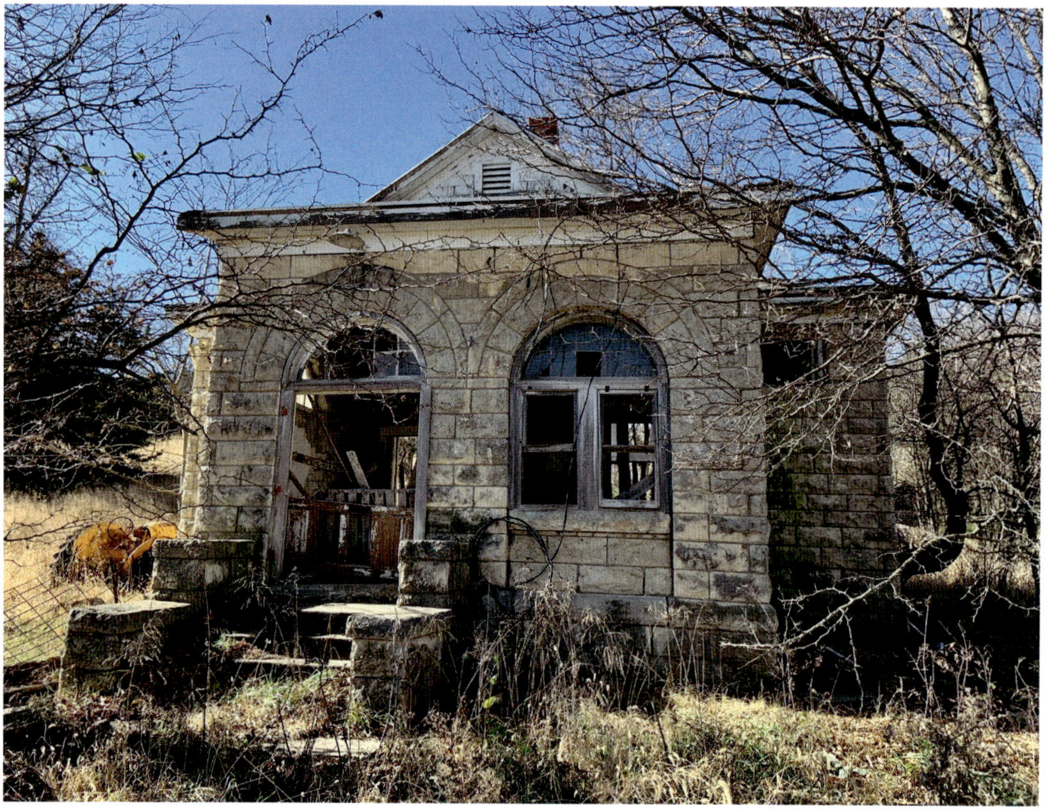

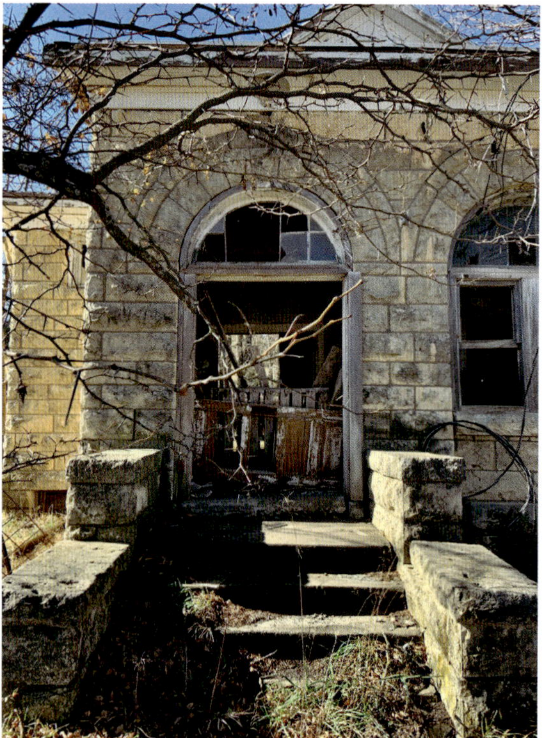

Above: Front of District 12 schoolhouse, also known as the Half Acre School. Located between Skiddy and Junction City, the one-room schoolhouse closed in the late 1950s, seen in November 2020.

Left: Front entrance to the Half Acre School, located between Skiddy and Junction City, November 2020.

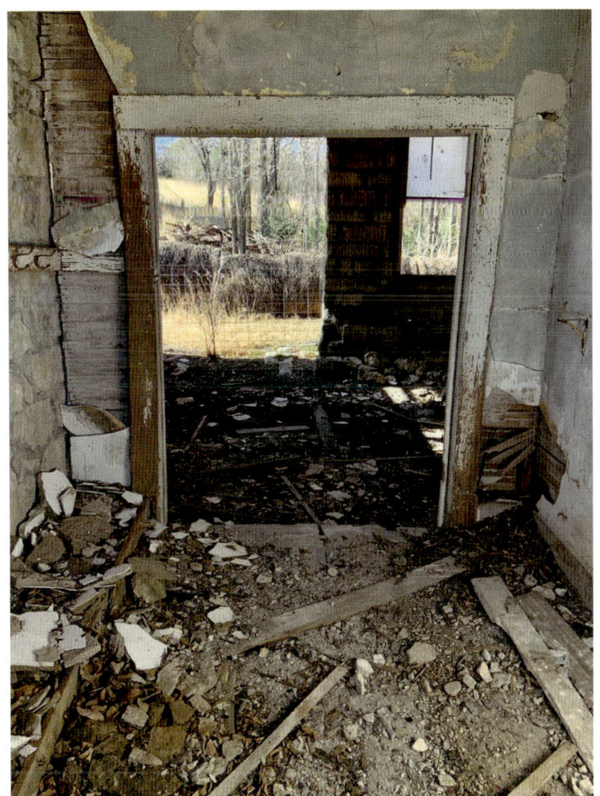

Right: Front entryway closet where the students would hang up their coats before sitting at their desks. The coat hooks are still on the left side wall inside the Half Acre School, located a few miles outside Skiddy, November 2020.

Below: The student's coat hooks inside the front entryway inside the Half Acre School, located a few miles outside Skiddy, November 2020.

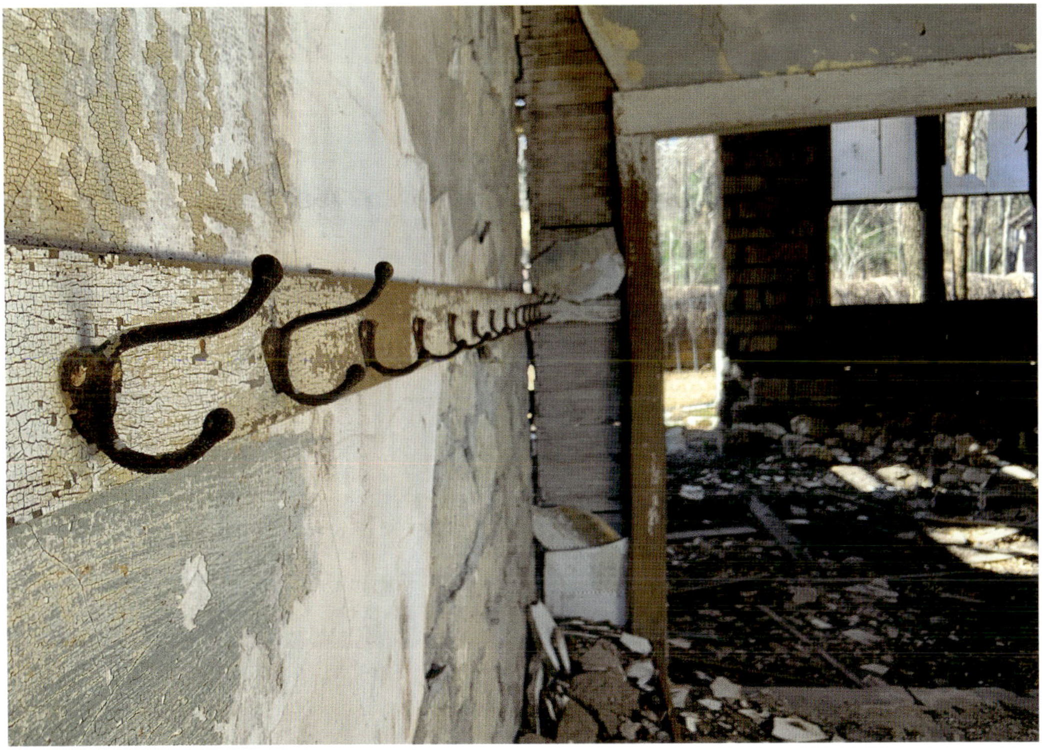

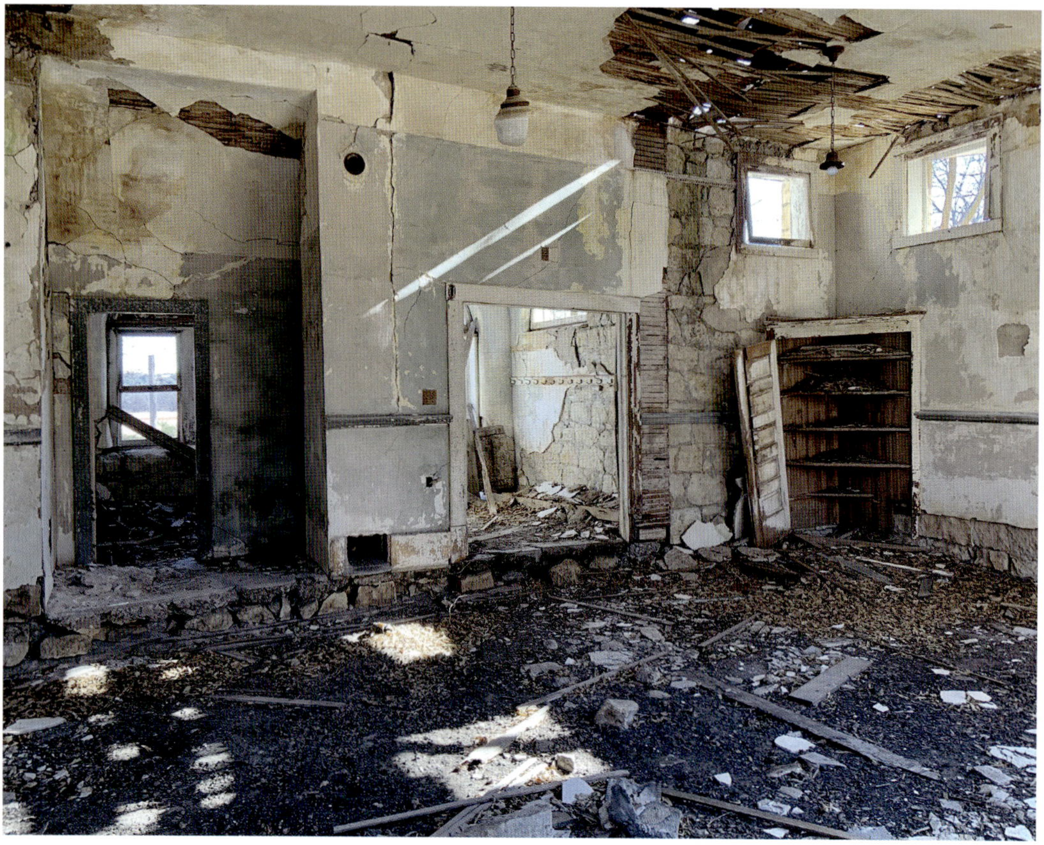

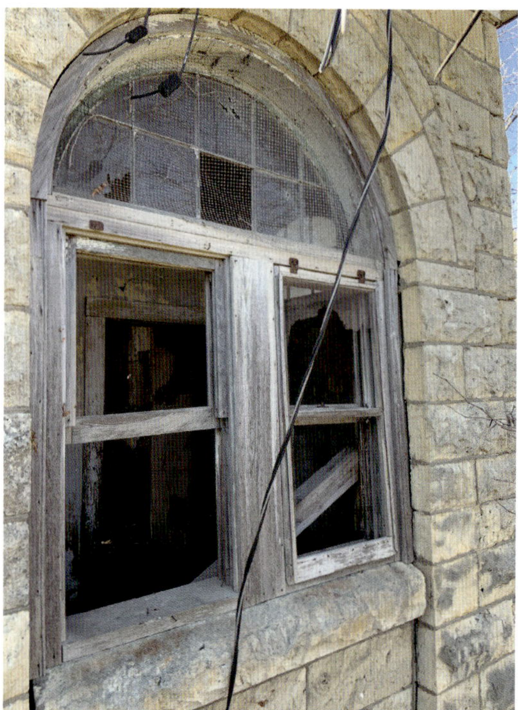

Above: Inside view of the Half Acre School. Although in bad shape and the one remaining door is falling off, the corner shelf continues to stand and a couple of light fixtures are still hanging from the ceiling inside the Half Acre School, located a few miles from Skiddy, November 2020.

Left: The windows are missing; however, the woodwork around the window frames of Half Acre School has held together well over the years, as seen in November 2020.

7

GREAT WESTERN PORTLAND CEMENT COMPANY

Another place that is really hidden in the trees was, at first glance, a lot of large concrete structures. Also, I did not realize how large it was until every time I thought it was the end, there was another section. It was upon further research that I discover this large factory was the Great Western Portland Cement Company. Sam McDermott, a businessman from Kansas City, bought acreage in the area that would later be known as the town of Mildred. In 1907, Sam had the cement factory built at the cost of $2 million, and the town was soon established out of necessity for those that worked in the factory. The town would be named after the daughter of J. W. Wagner, the company's president. The naming of the town would be called into question later the same year. When researching archived newspapers, I located an article from August 1907, stating that "We have heard it designated by two different names—Minneola and Mildred." Not sure how long after that article that Mildred was the decided-upon name but that became the town name. It also stated that Mildred, herself, did indeed visit the cement factory. While touring the factory, she lost her "fine gold watch" and it was never found.

The factory would go on to have 375 employees, and the town of Mildred would have 2,000 residents in the first few years of operation. In 1910, Great Western would hold the record for "producing more cement from one kiln in one day than any plant in the United States." In 1917, decreased demand for cement and increased costs of fuel meant the factory would close temporarily. Great Western did manage to partially reopen a short time later in the 1920s. Shortly after reopening, Great Western supplied the concrete for the construction of the Liberty Memorial, "the nation's official World War I memorial" located in Kansas City, Missouri. Construction for the 217-foot-tall memorial began in July 1923 and was complete and open in 1926.

Despite the partial reopening, the factory would permanently close in 1931. The factory closing started the decline of Mildred. Many started moving away in search of work, and local businesses suffered from the loss of revenue. Since that time, the town has a small handful of residents still lives in town and nature has slowly reclaimed the remaining concrete structures from the Great Western Cement Company, except for the storage silos that sit right on the roadside.

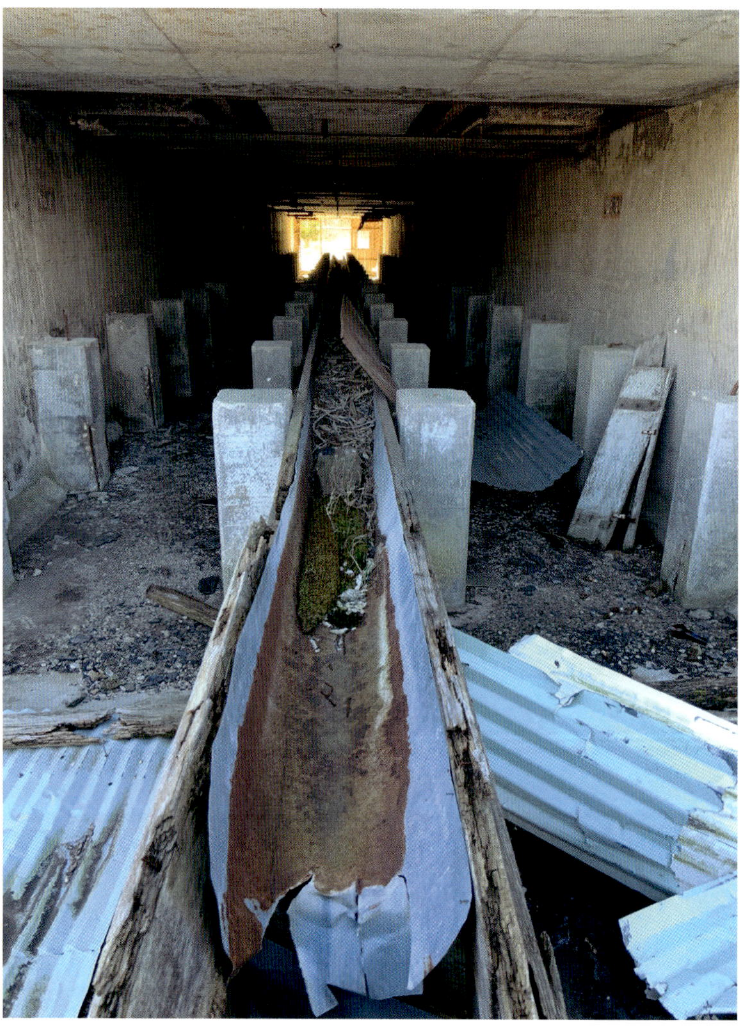

A view into the conveyer belt area under the concrete storage silos at the Great Western Portland Cement Company, outside Mildred, November 2020.

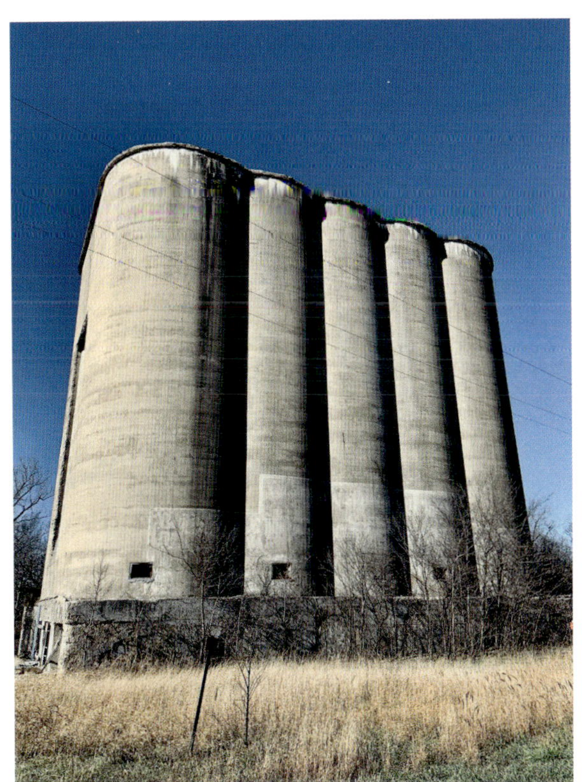

The concrete storage towers for the Great Western Portland Cement Company, sit just a few feet from the highway, just outside the town of Mildred.

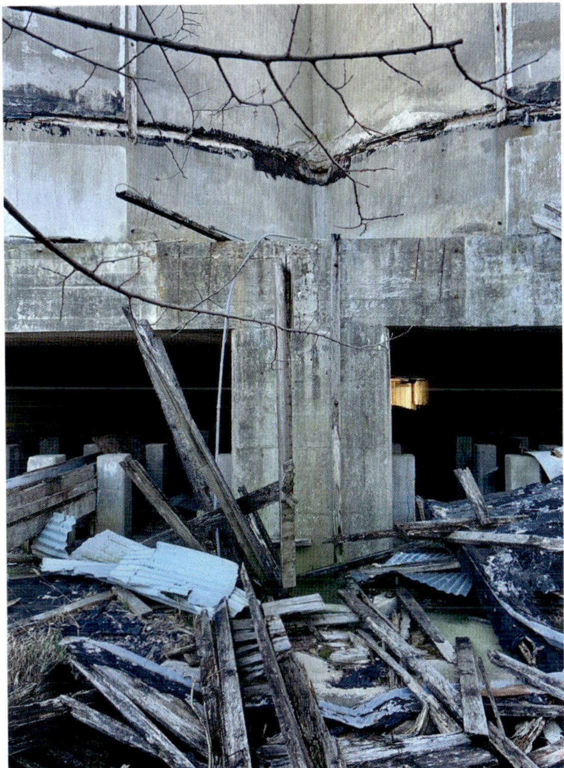

Underneath the storage silos for the Great Western Portland Cement Company, is where the rocks were dispensed onto conveyor belts, located outside Mildred, November 2020.

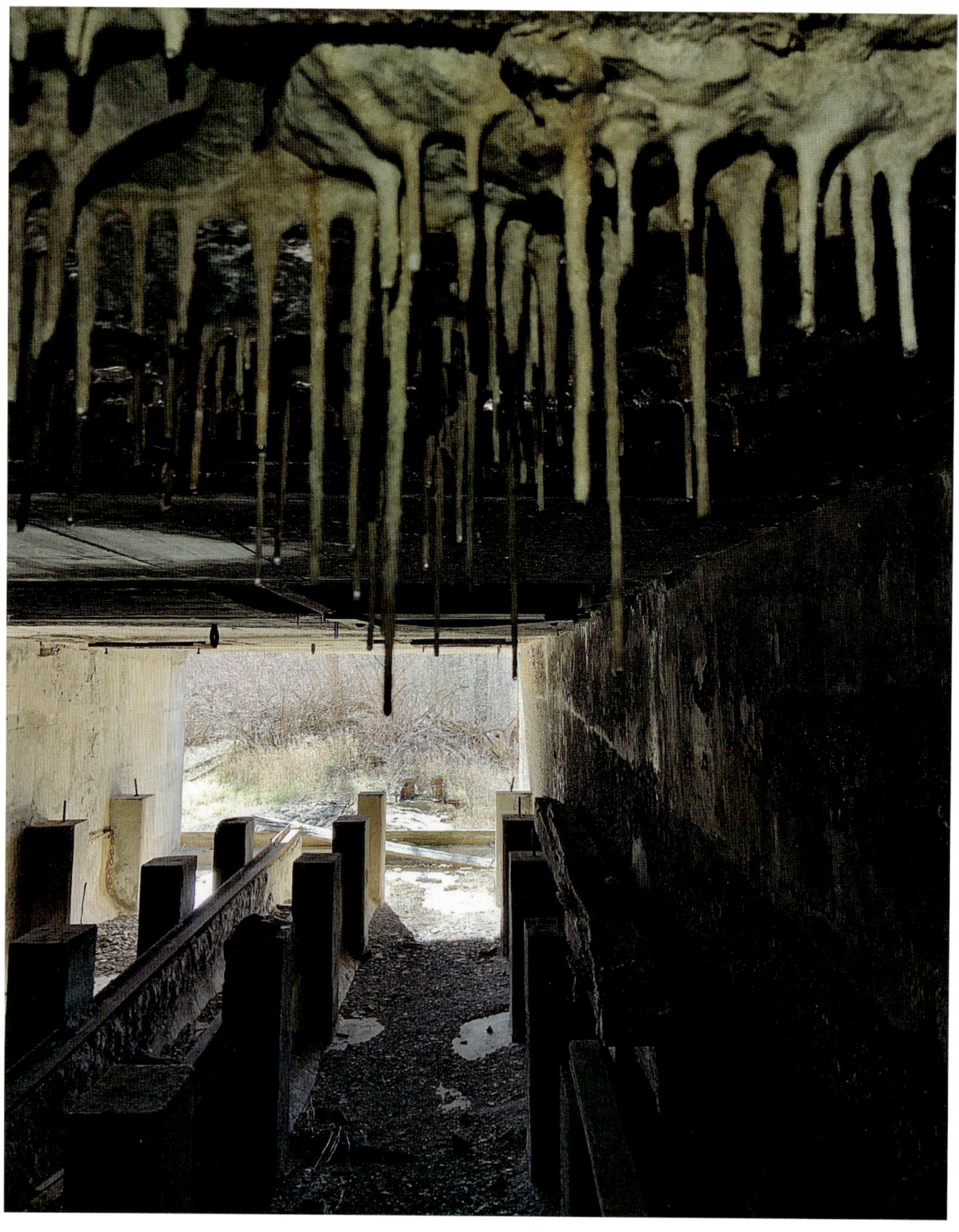

Stalactites hang from the top of the dispensing area underneath the storage silos at the Great Western Portland Cement Company, located outside Mildred, November 2020.

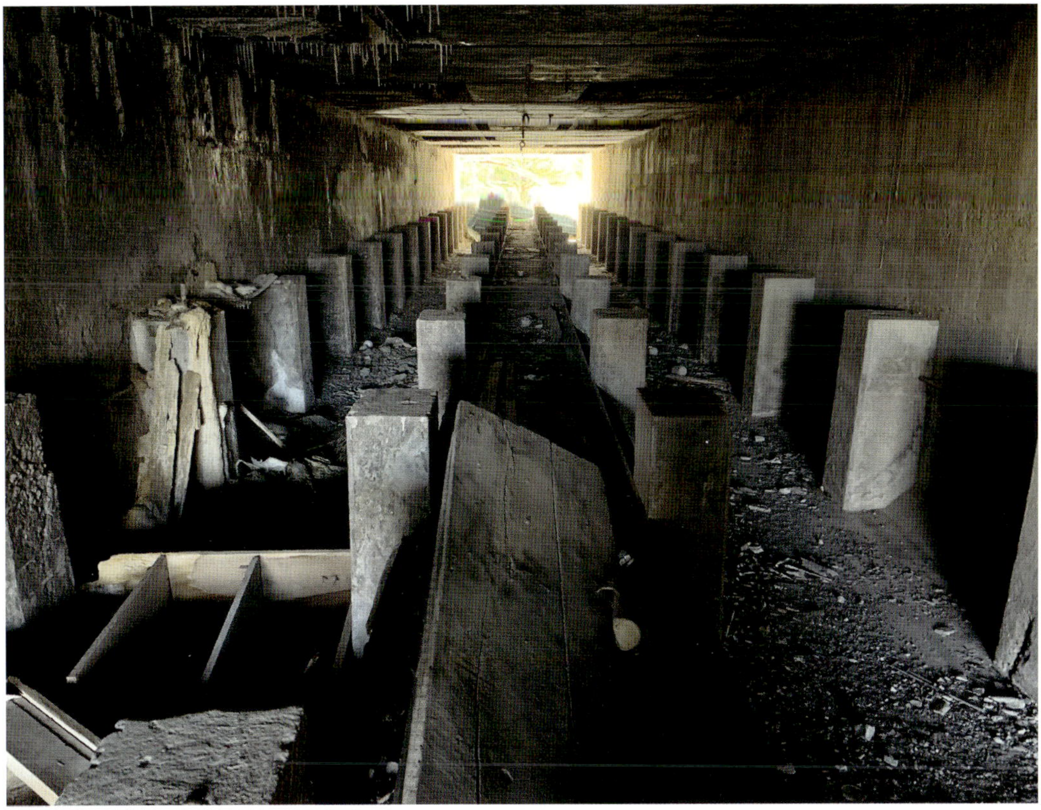

Above: View down the next conveyer belt tunnel underneath the storage silos at the Great Western Portland Cement, located outside Mildred, November 2020.

Right: Looking up the ladder into the concrete silos at the Great Western Portland Cement, located outside Mildred, November 2020.

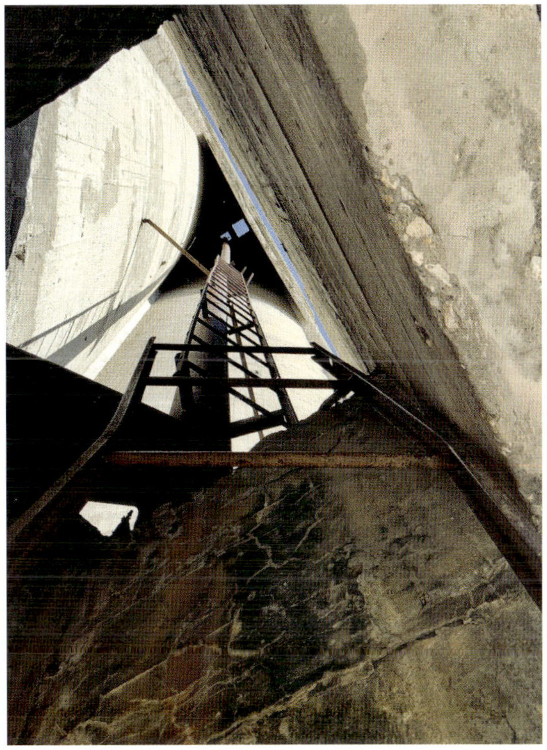

Starting from the silos, the grounds of the factory stretch back around 300 yards. Tall concrete structures, stairs, and short tunnels are in each section of the former factory. Standing atop of a few places, you can see over the trees and an overall view of what is left of that section. I am glad that I explored the old cement factory in the later part of the year when the surrounding forest is dead and critters are hibernating. The thick overgrowth was slightly difficult to navigate through in November. It would be doubly harder when vegetation and trees are flourishing. Besides the Kansas Department of Health and Environment taking efforts throughout 1999 to 2000, to clean up the years of illegal trash dumping, I could not locate any city or county plans for the Greater Western Portland Cement Company.

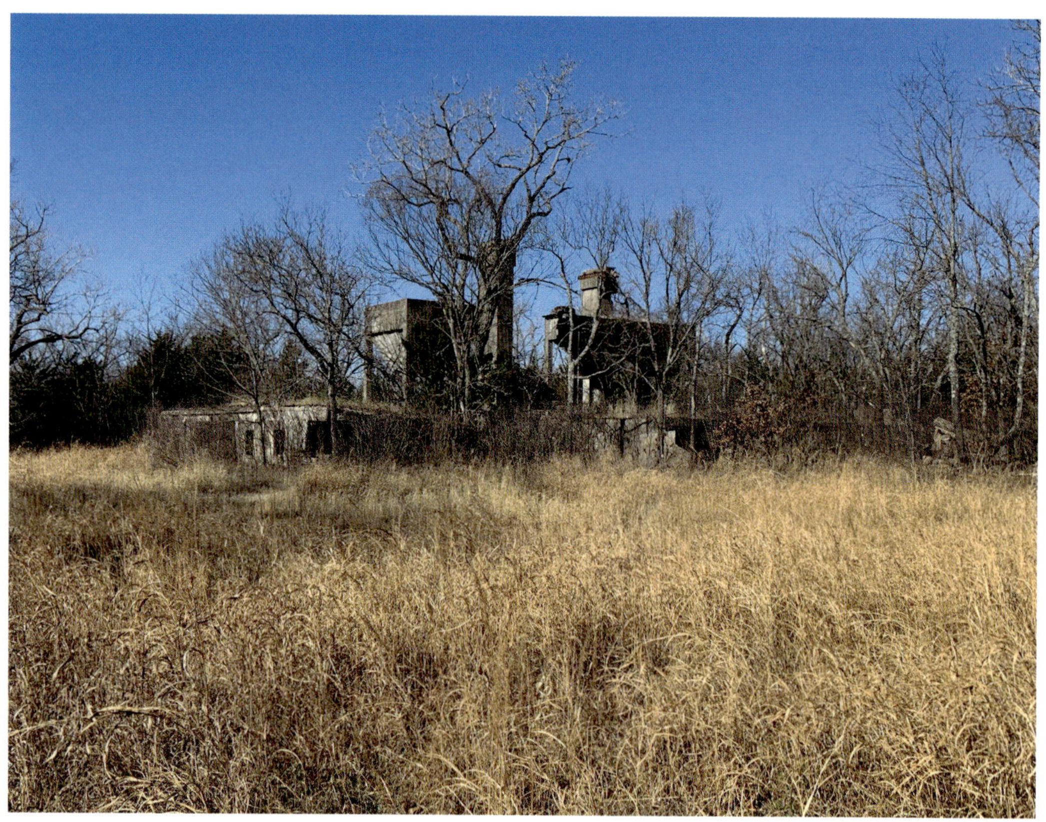

Beyond the concrete silos and through the trees is the rest of the Great Western Portland Cement Company, outside Mildred in November 2020. Even in fall, the rest of what remains is still very camouflaged by the surrounding trees.

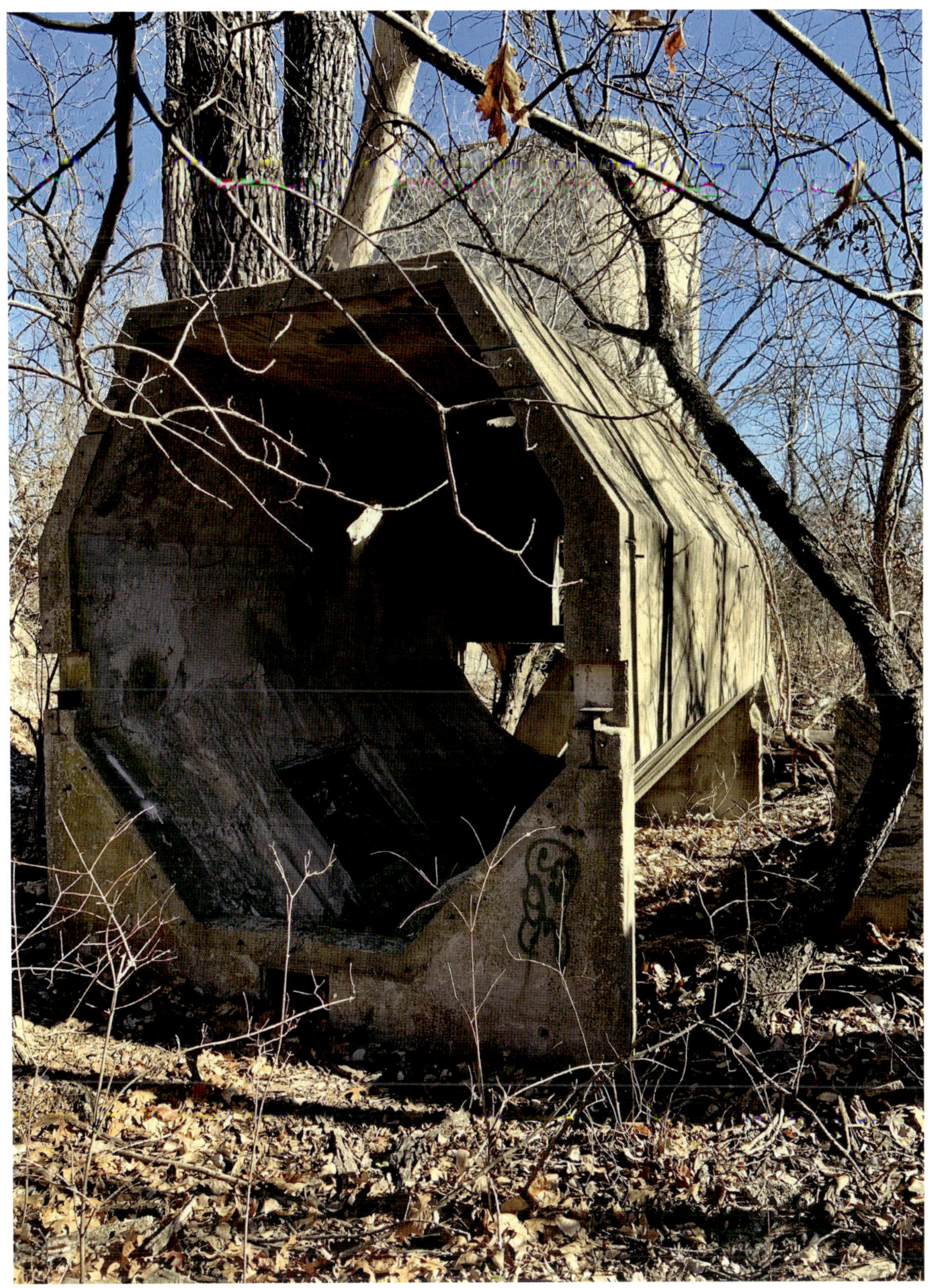

Part of a concrete structure at the Great Western Portland Cement Company, outside Mildred, November 2020.

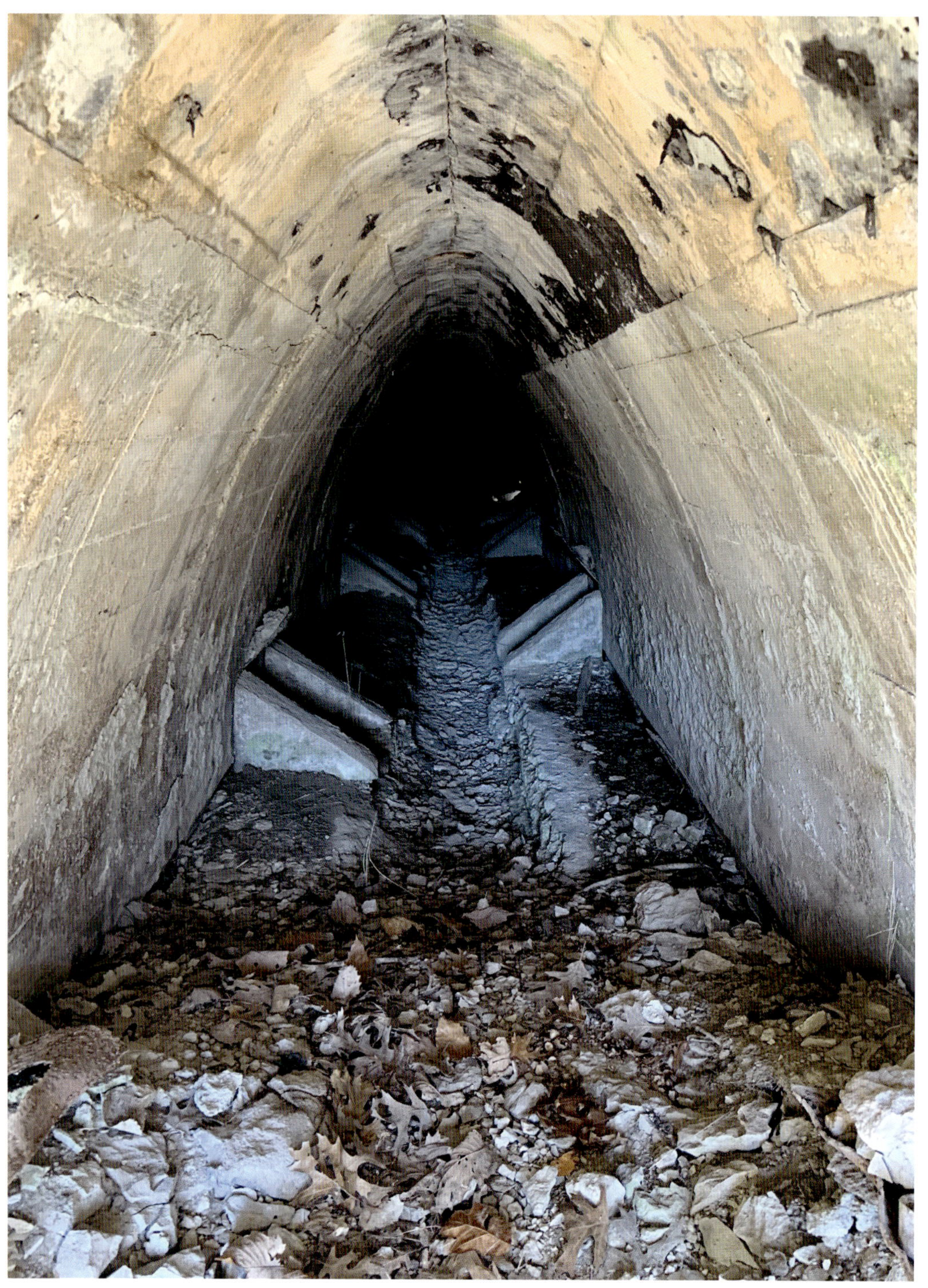

Inside of the tunnels at the Great Western Portland Cement Company, outside Mildred, November 2020.

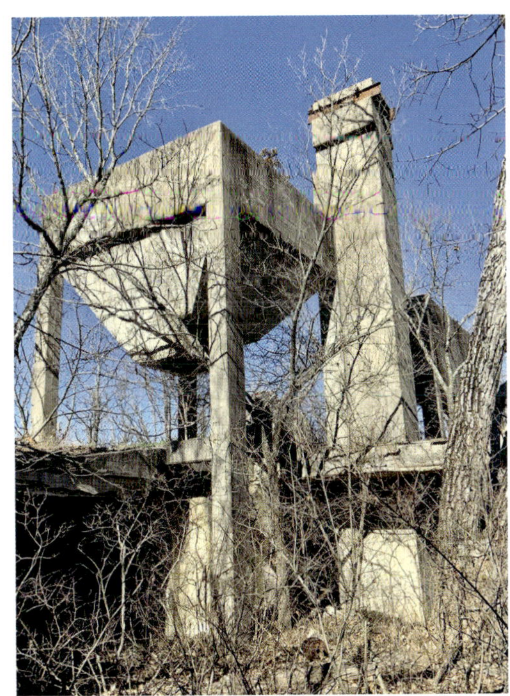

Right: Part of the Great Western Portland Cement Company factory hidden in the woods outside Mildred, November 2020.

Below: Another part of the Great Western Portland Cement Company factory hidden in the woods outside Mildred, November 2020.

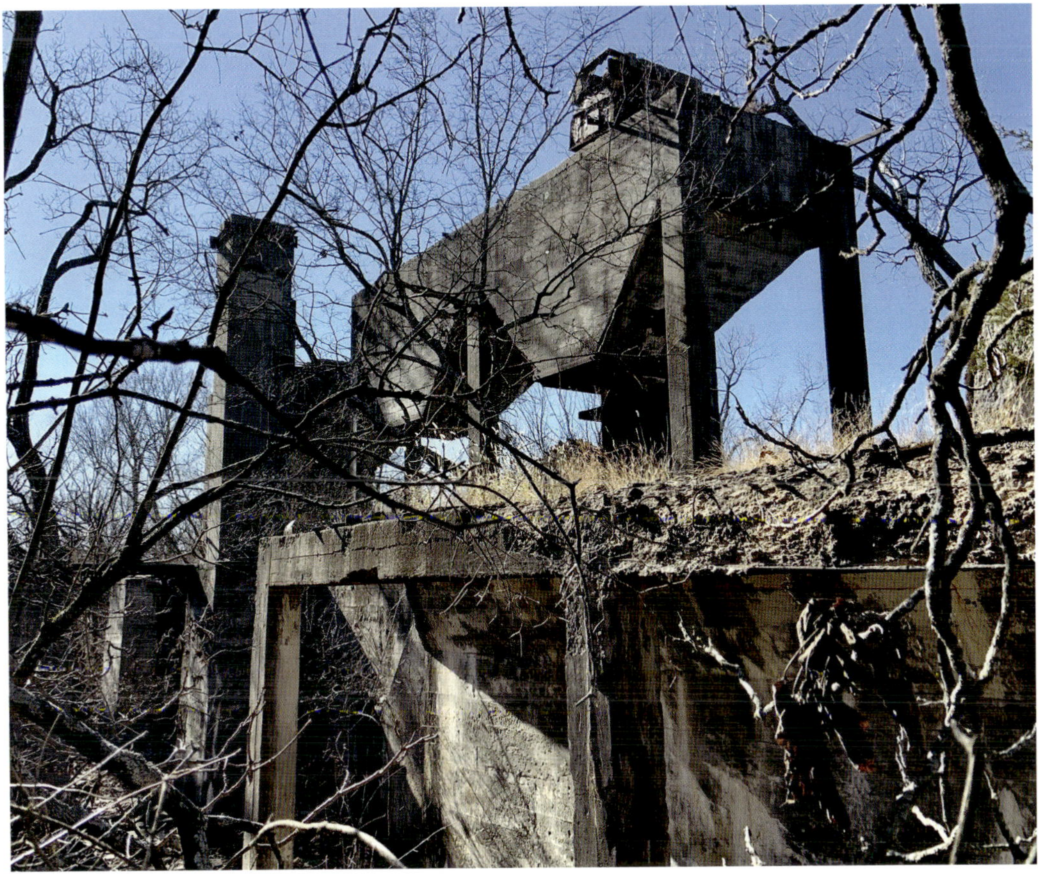

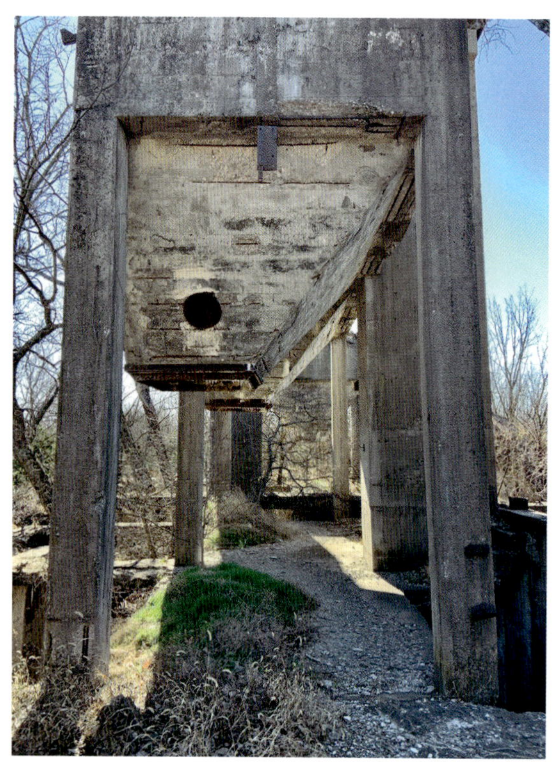

Left: Standing up top of one of the tall remaining structures at the Great Western Portland Cement Company outside Mildred, November 2020.

Below: Standing on one of the tall structures, you can see some of the remaining Great Western Portland Cement Company below. Much of the rest is hidden by all the trees. Located outside Mildred, November 2020.

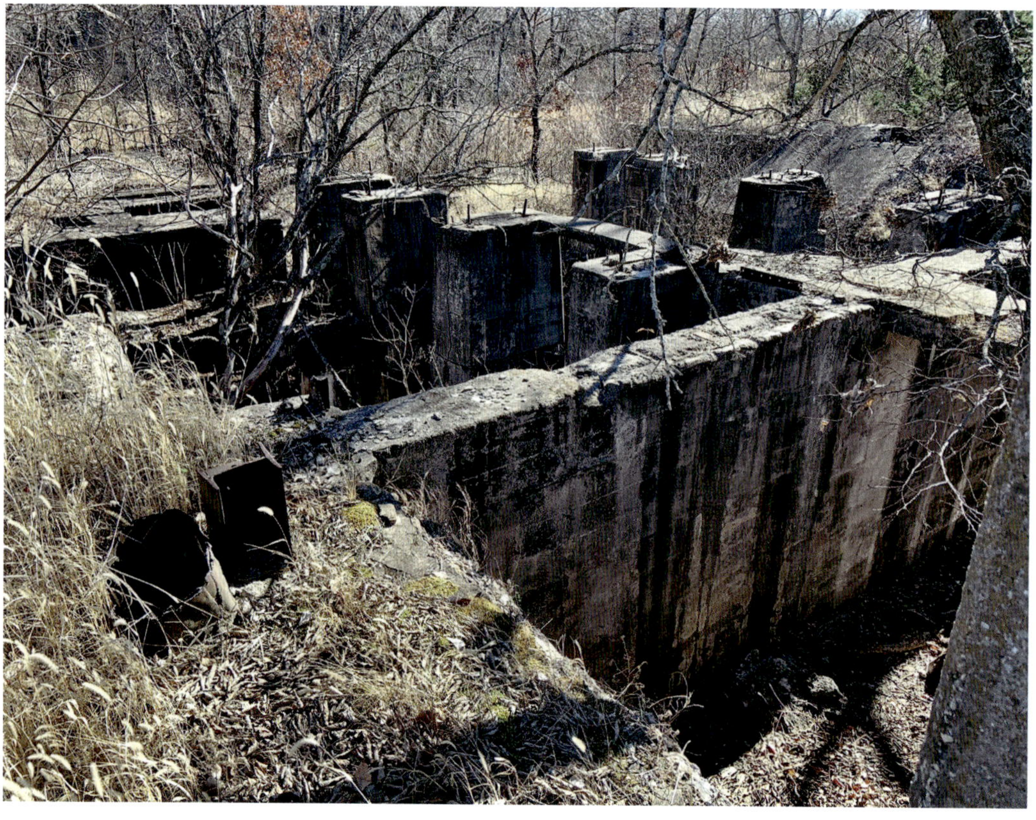

8

NEOSHO FALLS

NEOSHO FALLS POPULATION: 104 (2019)

A higher population of people live in Neosho Falls than the other towns talked about in this book. However, many of the buildings throughout town are abandoned, mostly collapsed, and being reclaimed by nature. The history of this town tells a discouraging story of taking two steps forward to take even more steps back.

The oldest town in Woodson County, Neosho Falls was founded in 1857 and named after the river that the town sits next to. Construction and establishment would happen very quickly in the first few years. A dam was built across the river, and a short time later, one of the town's earliest settlers built a sawmill on the river. The sawmill's job opportunities brought settlers to the area, and a year later, Neosho Falls was becoming more established, with the opening of a store, pharmacy, and the Falls House Hotel.

The town continued to grow over the years, ushering in more changes to accommodate the increasing population. The first public school would start construction in 1869, and the children of Neosho Falls would start attending school the following year. In addition to the school opening, the next couple of years would bring much change for Neosho Falls. The town would become incorporated, making way for their first bank, as well as a depot stop on the KATY Railway. City official elections would take place, and construction of the first church and the Falls House Hotel and renovations on the high school for expansion took place.

Even with the opening of a new wool mill on the opposite side of the river in 1873, Neosho Falls would suffer a big loss when the town's bank closed. Three years later, more closures happened when one of the town's newer hotels, the

American Hotel, would close their doors and the Pierce House Hotel sustained serious damage from a fire.

Neosho Falls would see improvements throughout the 1880s, with the improvements being made to Grist Mill and the arrival of a new town bank. In the early part of the 1900s, the mills would close due to electricity being utilized over water power, the closure of the electric facility, a catastrophic flood in 1926, the Great Depression, and important business losses into the 1930s. The discovery of oil close to town brought a little bit of life back to Neosho Falls, and a new school would be built. However, another flood in 1951 left the town in ruins, and the KATY Railway no longer operated in the area, causing more of the town's residents to move away. Eventually, the high school would close in 1961 and the elementary school in 1969.

Today, many of the town's buildings are abandoned and slowly deteriorating, and there are not nearly as many residents as before. There is still standing history all over Neosho Falls, from the last high school the town had built to the riverside powerhouse. Despite all the changes and devastation over its history, the waterfall on the Neosho River, the town's namesake, has remained unchanged over the years and is the highlight of Neosho Falls.

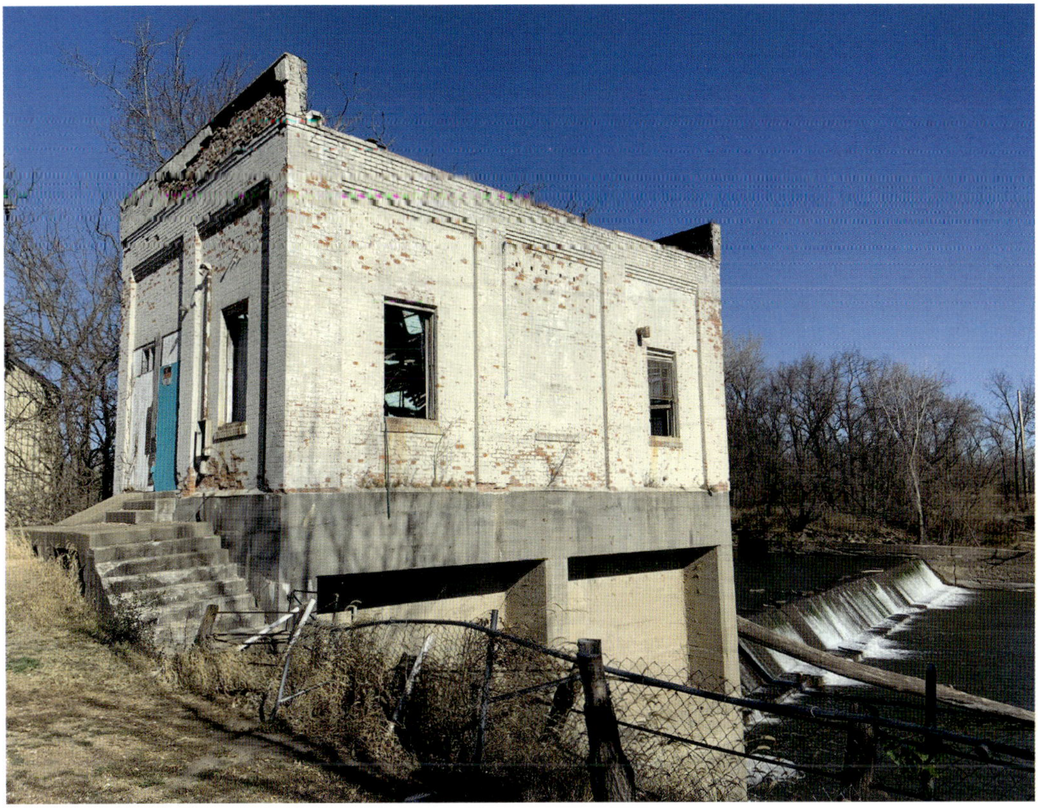

Above: Riverside powerhouse and the waterfall on the Neosho River, located in Neosho Falls, November 2020.

Right: View through the boards that are over the windows at the collapsing riverside powerhouse in Neosho Falls, November 2020.

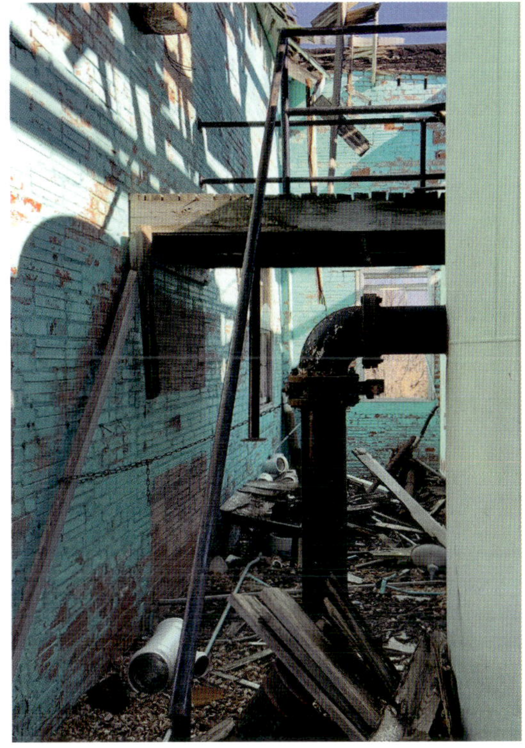

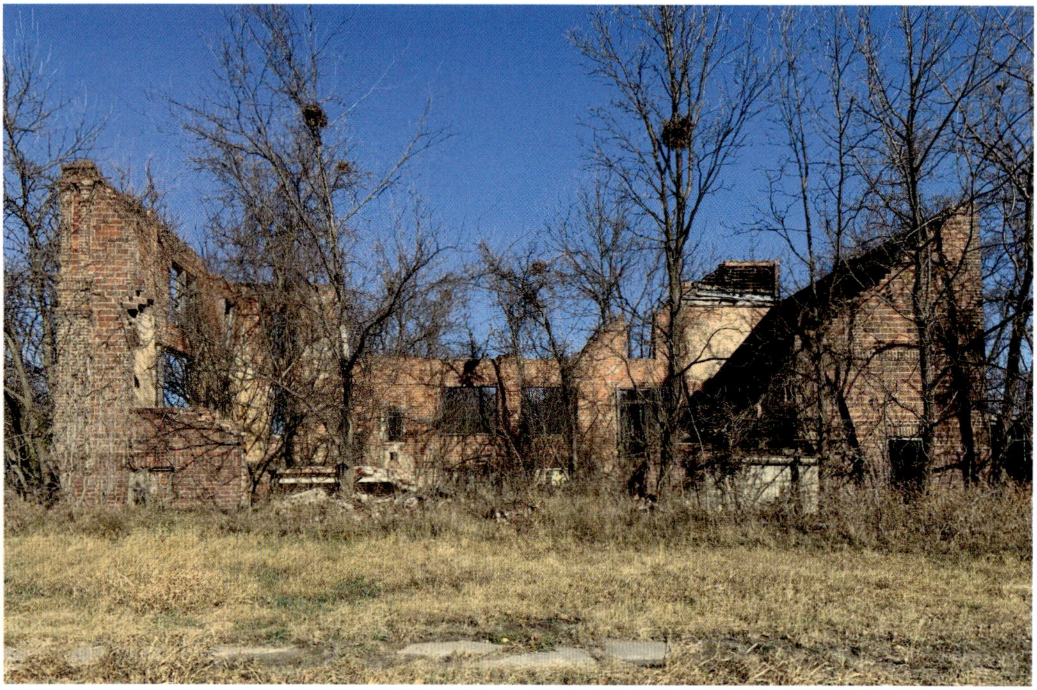

This collapsed and abandoned brick building is being reclaimed by the surrounding trees, located in Neosho Falls, November 2020.

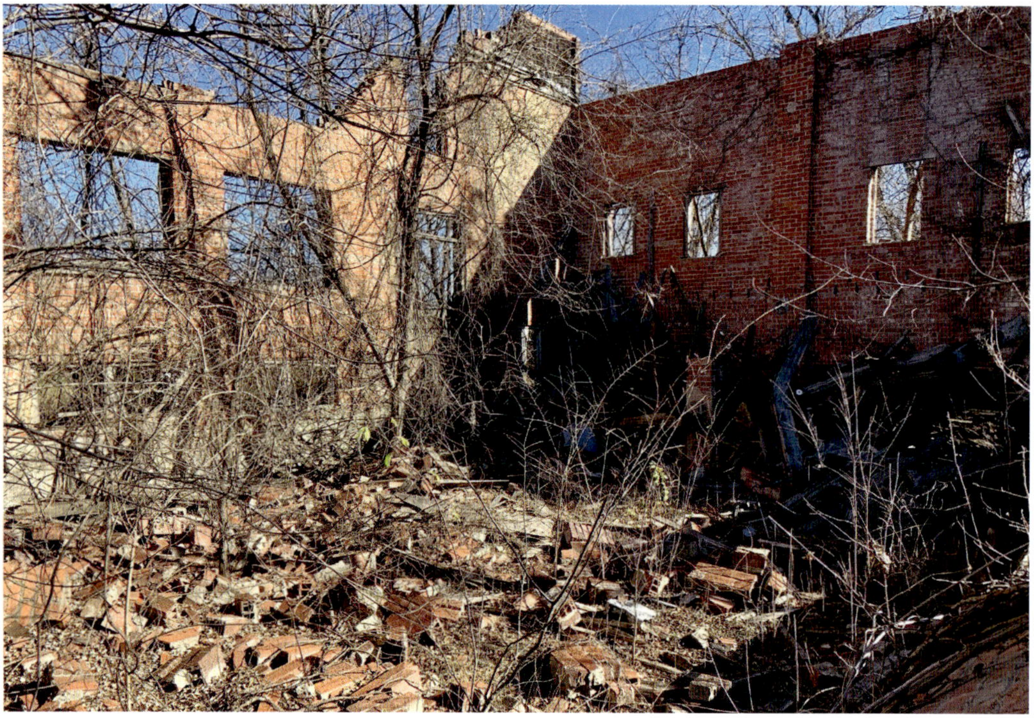

A look inside the collapsed brick building. There are trees growing inside as well as the outside, located in Neosho Falls, November 2020.

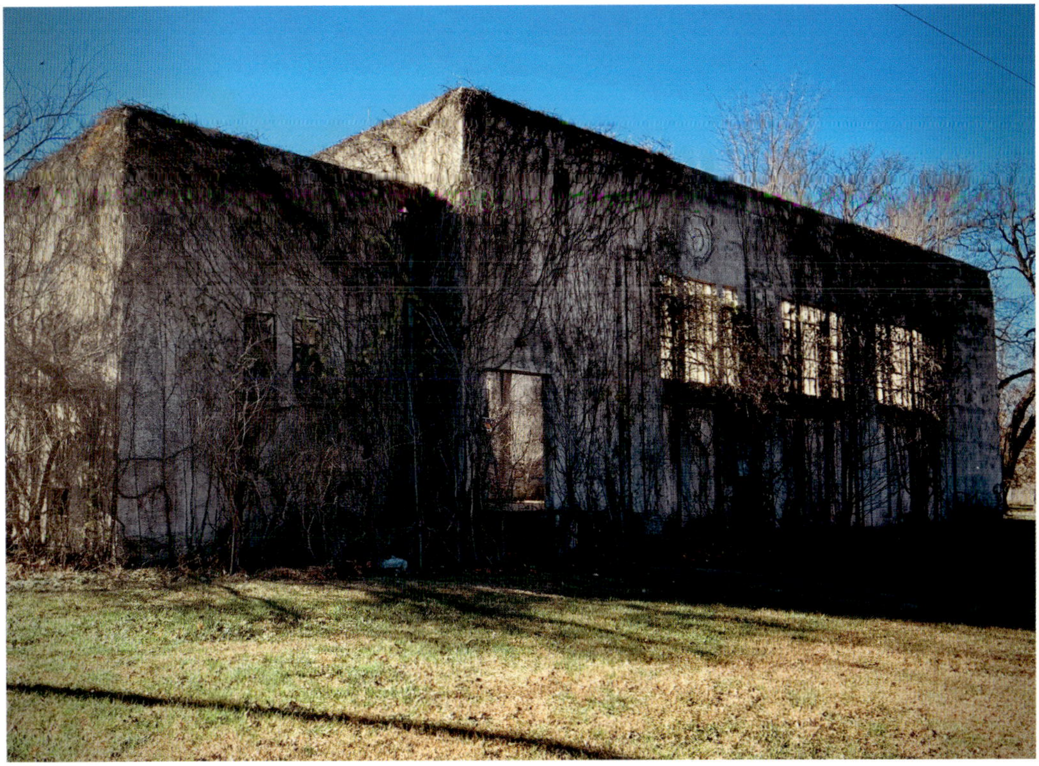

Above: Closed since 1961, the Neosho Falls High School is now covered in vines, November 2020.

Right: A tree growing inside the abandoned high school in Neosho Falls, November 2020.

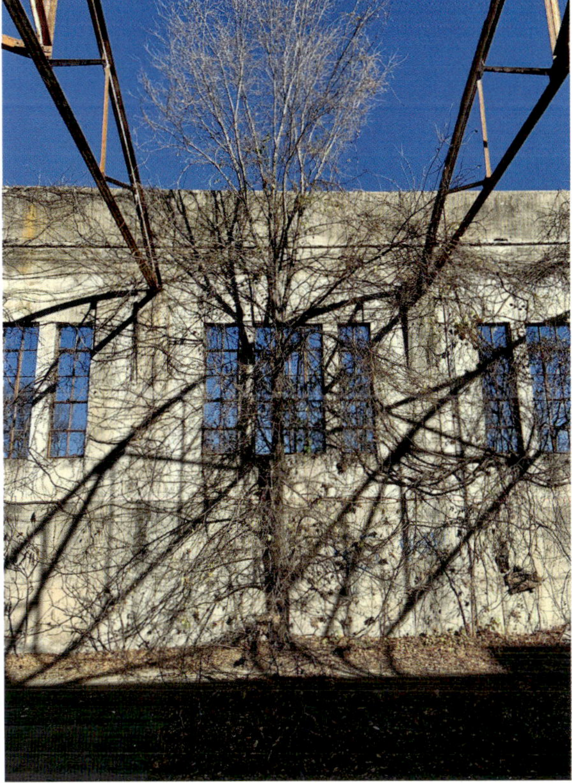

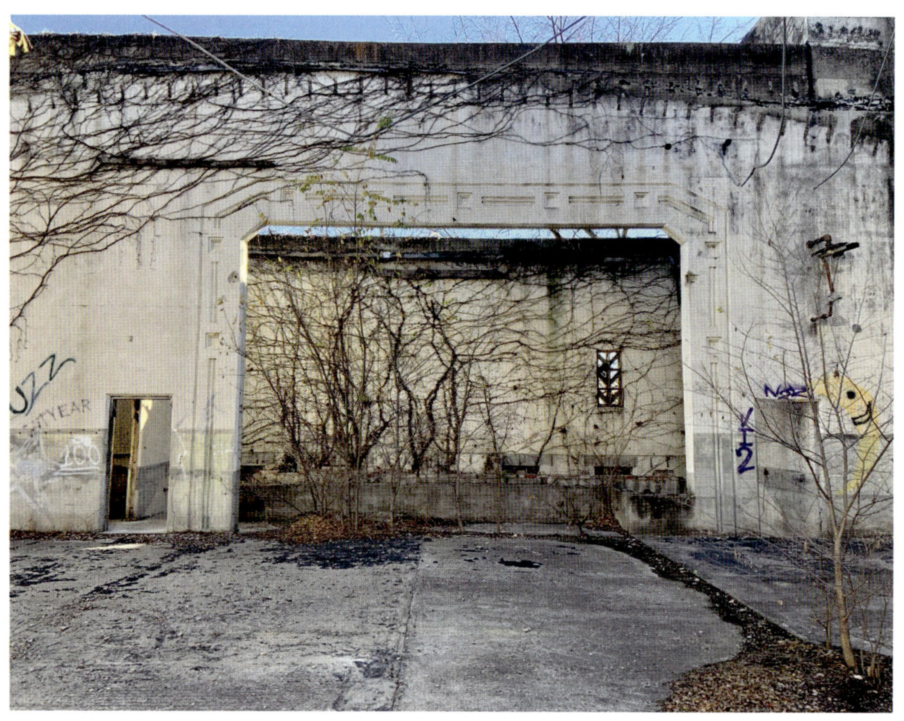

The stage in the auditorium in the high school in Neosho Falls, November 2020.

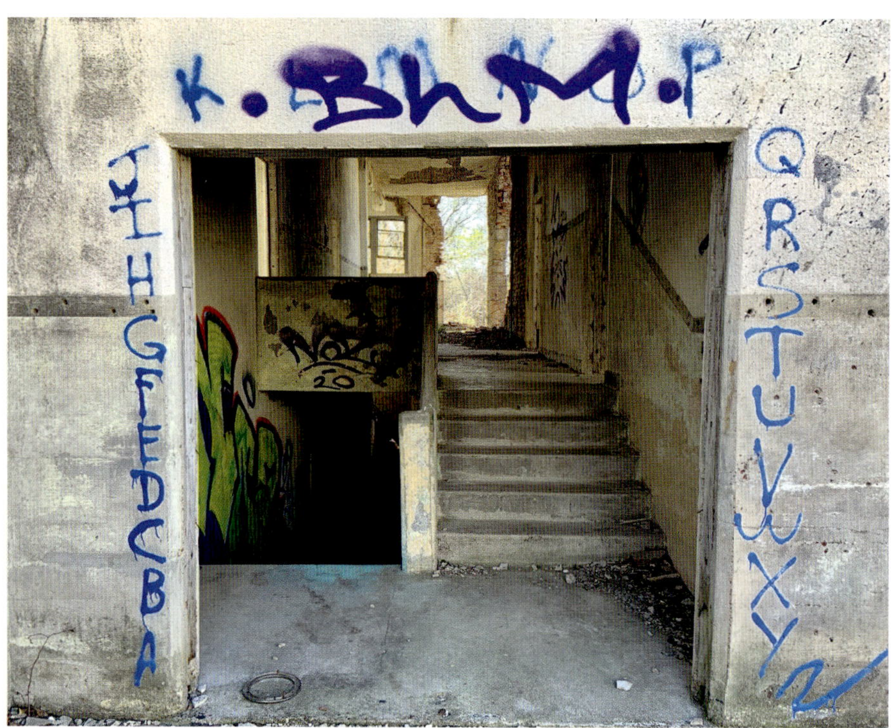

View down one of the halls from the auditorium in the high school in Neosho Falls, November 2020.

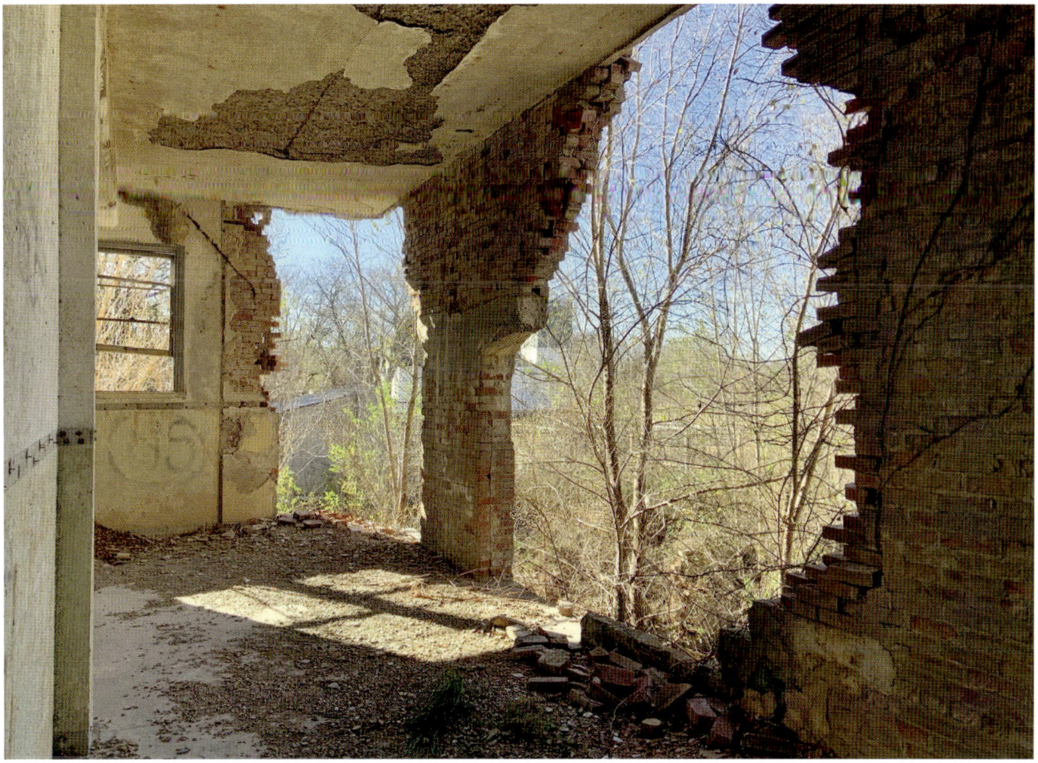

Part of the wall on the second floor has either had bricks removed or they have fallen off over the years, located in Neosho Falls, November 2020.

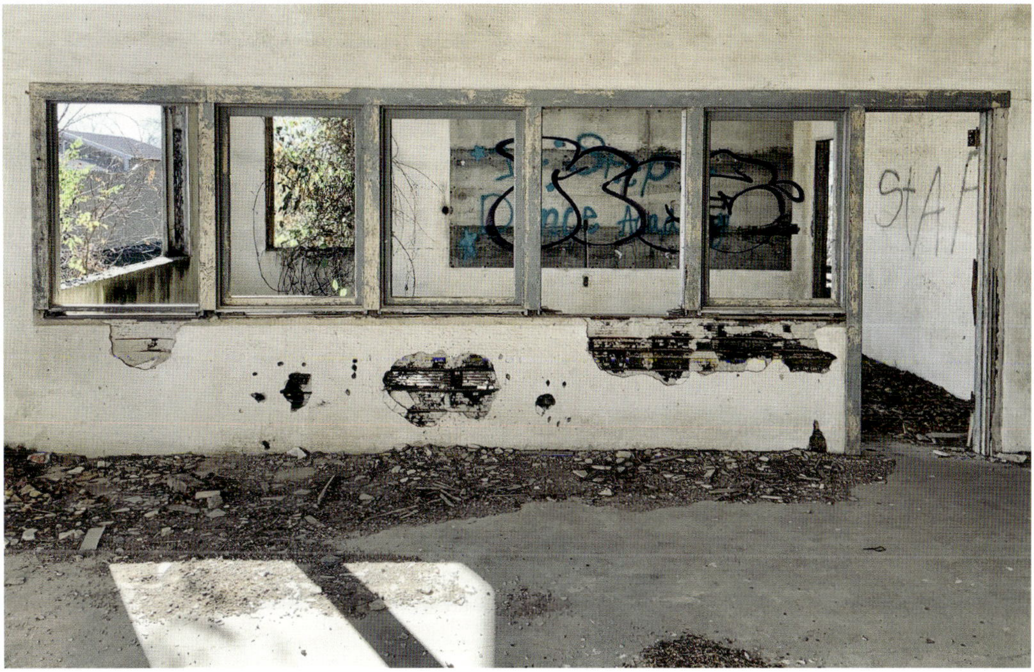

The view from one classroom into another inside the high school in Neosho Falls, November 2020.

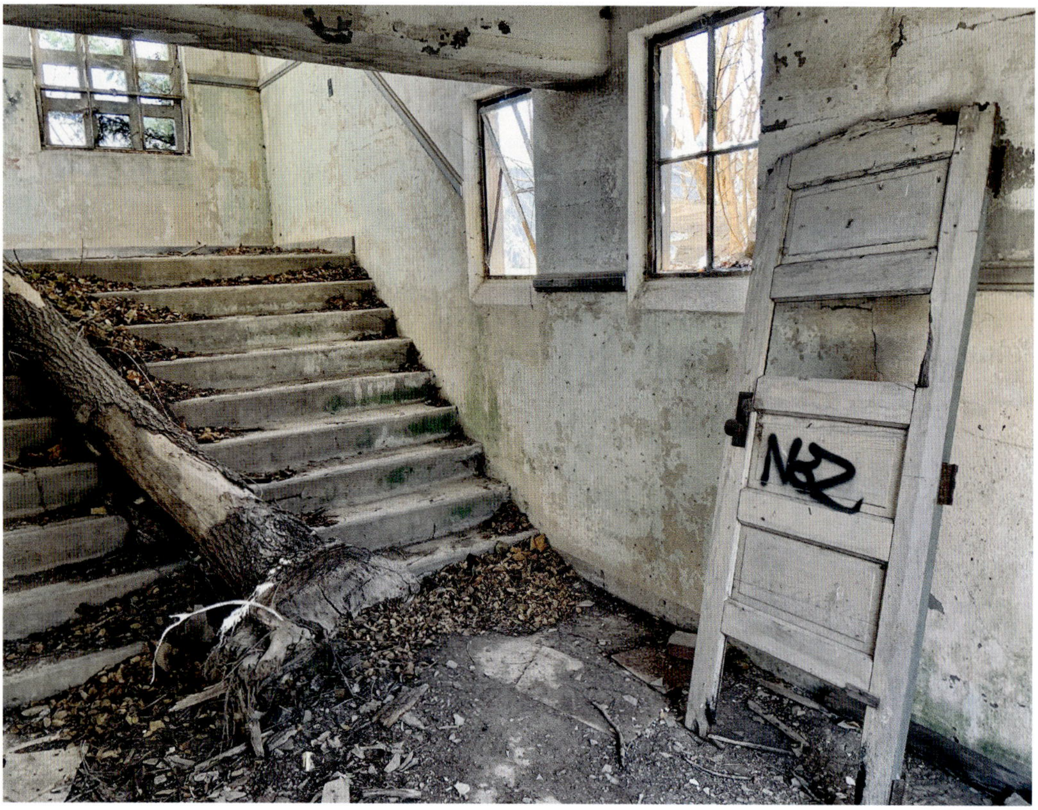

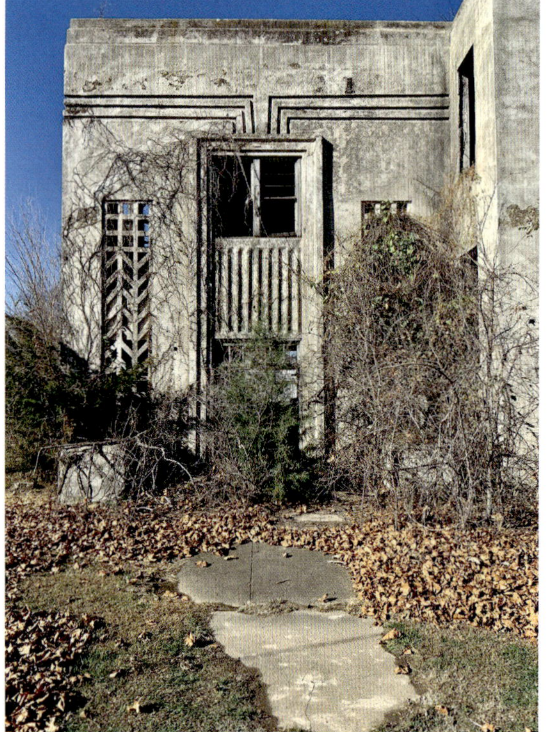

Above: A large tree lays on the stairs in the high school in Neosho Falls, November 2020.

Left: Despite being closed since the 1960s and covered in trees and vines, you can still see the design work on the outside of the high school in Neosho Falls, November 2020.

Kansas, many times is seen as a pass-through state that, outside the few big cities, is a vast frontier of farms and the flatlands of the Great Plains. At first glance of the countryside and ghost towns of Kansas, it does appear to be the epitome of "the middle of nowhere," but when you detour off the main road, the back road ghost towns and small forgotten places have many stories to tell.

All of these places were once so full of life, each one giving structure and support to the establishment of the town and its people. Such as life, the purpose and opportunity of these places ran their courses, leaving behind skeletal structures of a life once lived, a purpose once served and a story to be heard. These skeletons of the Sunflower State are merely the tip of the iceberg of how truly historic the small towns and places in between are to the establishments throughout Kansas and the Midwest.

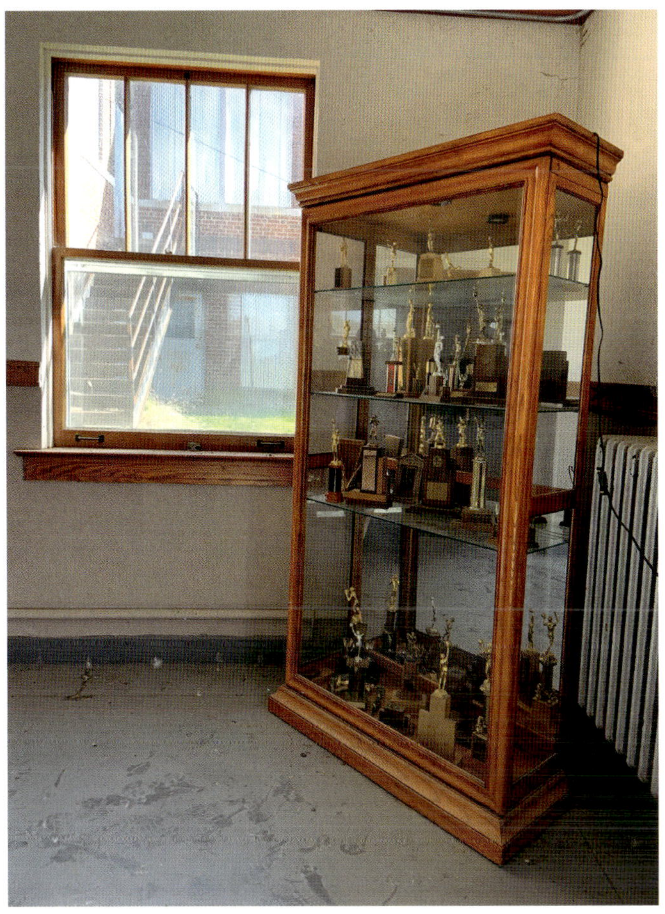

Trophy case full of trophies in a school in Cedar Point, April 2020.

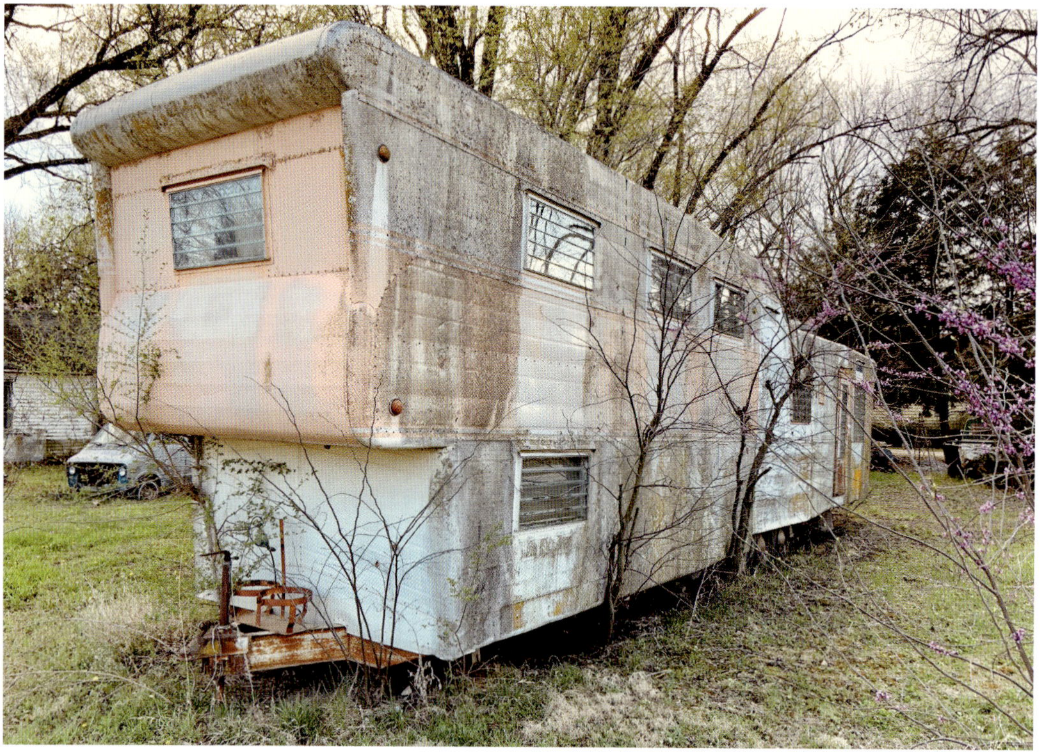

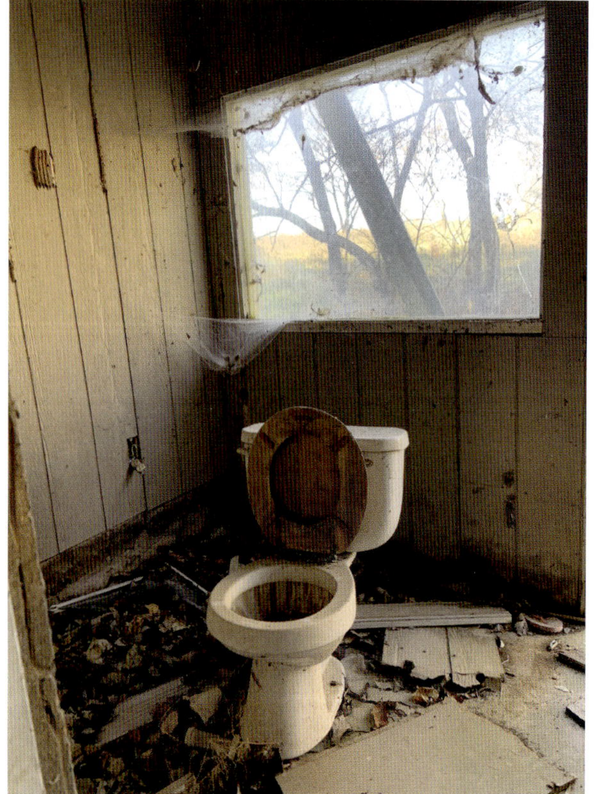

Above: An abandoned trailer in Elmdale, April 2020.

Left: Toilet found on the porch of this abandoned house outside Paola, November 2020.

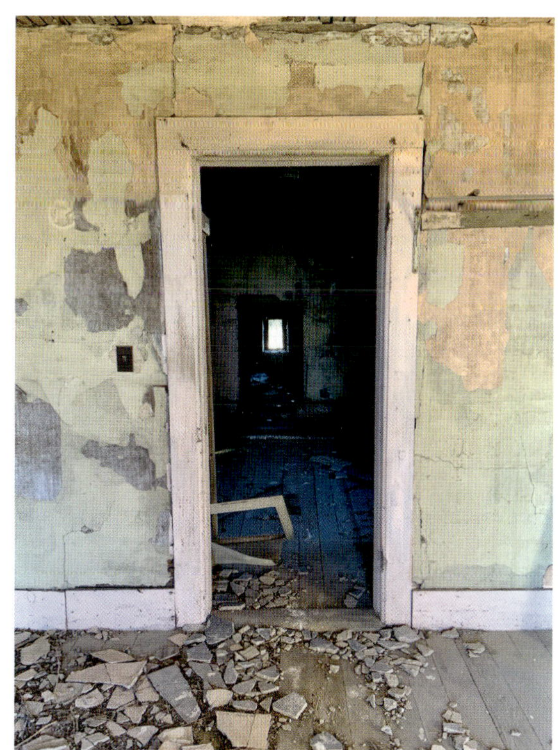

Right: The walls and ceiling are slowly crumbling in this abandoned house outside Ottawa, November 2020.

Below: An abandoned pool table in a collapsing building in Williamsburg, November 2020.

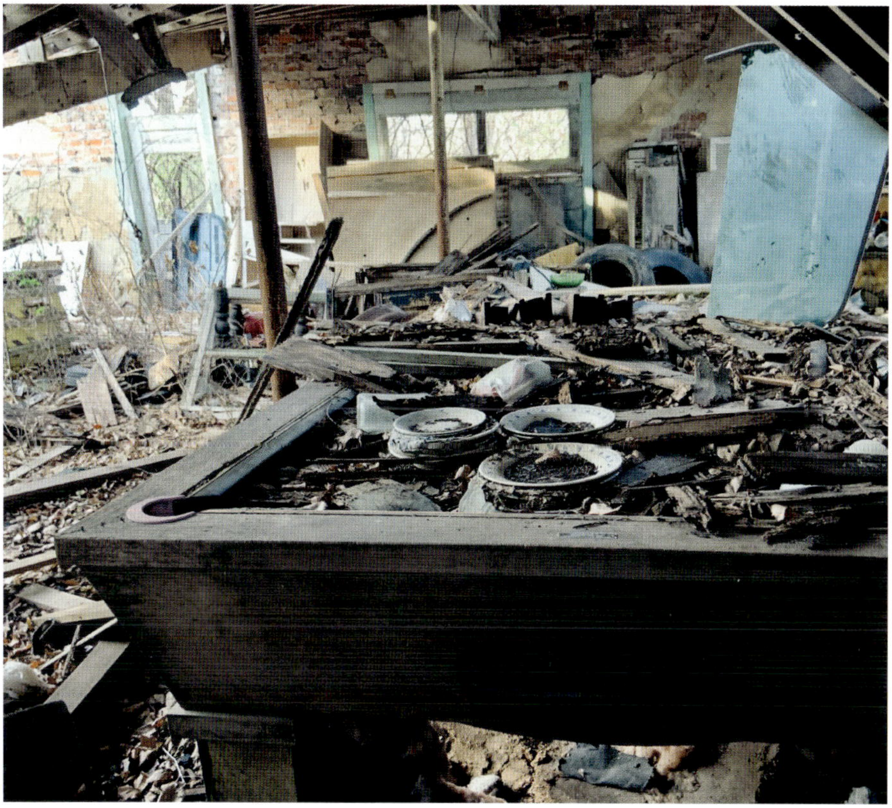

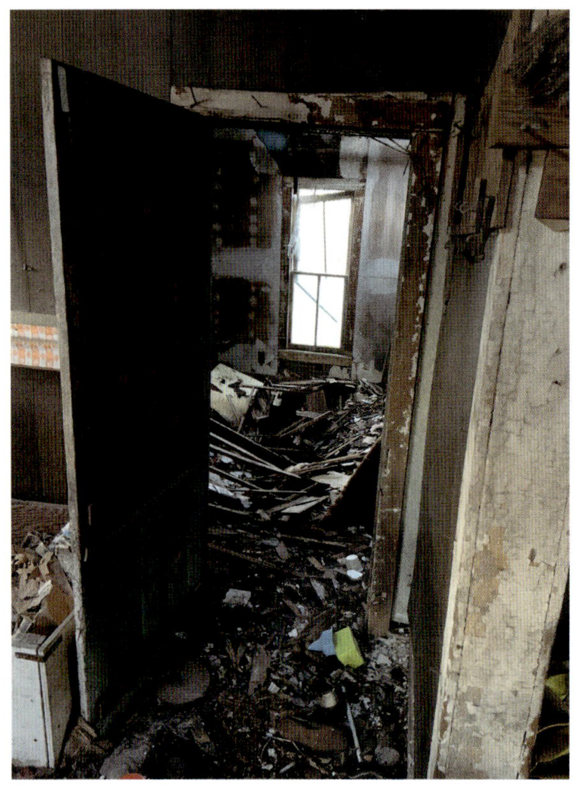

The floor is collapsing in this abandoned house outside Lyndon, November 2020.

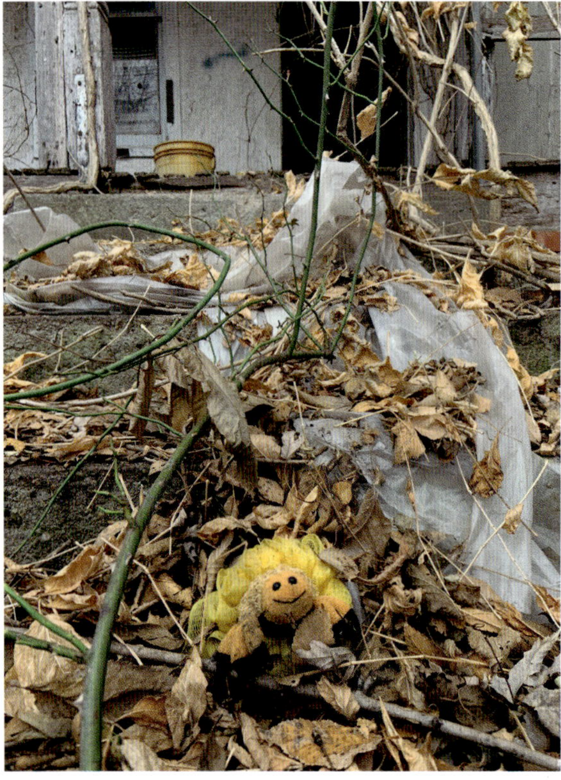

Such a welcoming smile from this bath toy found on the steps of an abandoned house in Dunlap, November 2020.

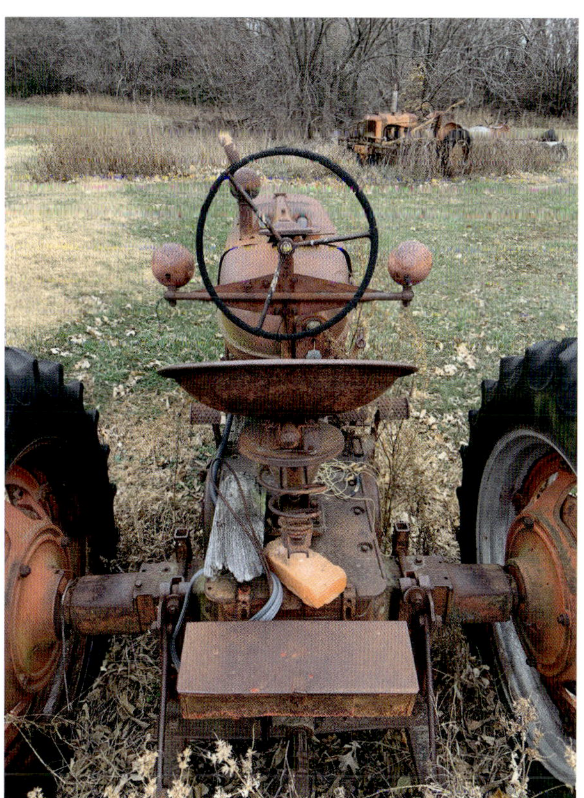

Right: A couple of abandoned tractors in Americus, November 2020.

Below: One of the few pieces of graffiti I found on the whole trip throughout Eastern Kansas. This was on the wall of one of the classrooms in the high school in Bushong, November 2020.

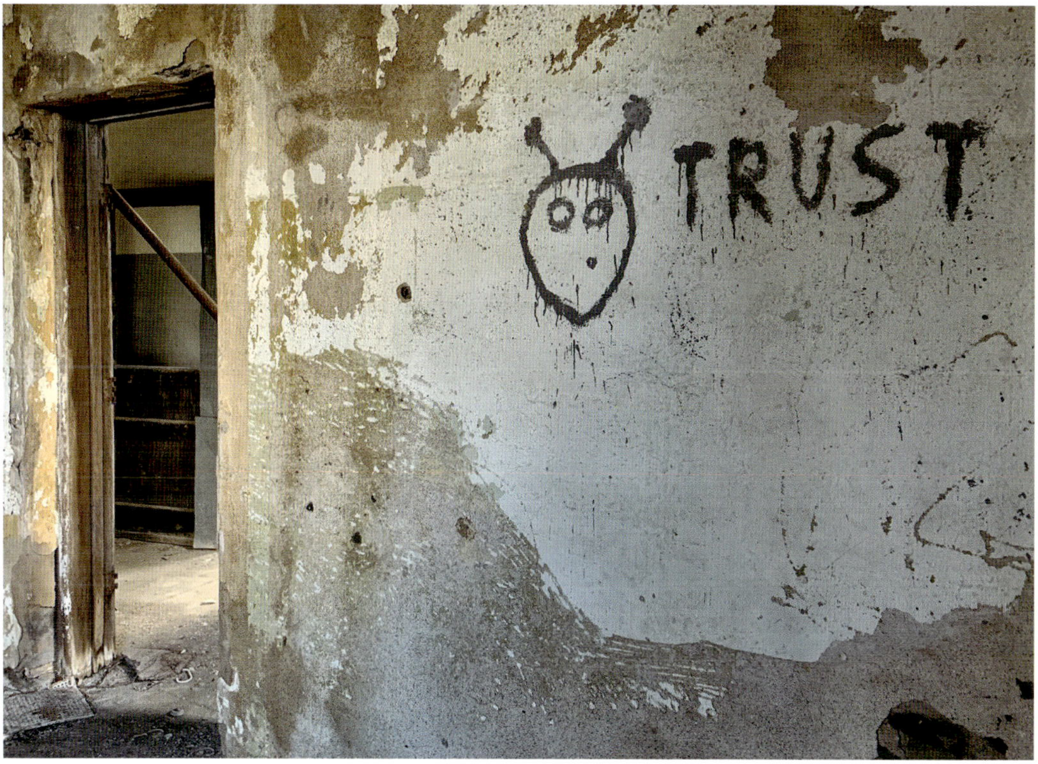

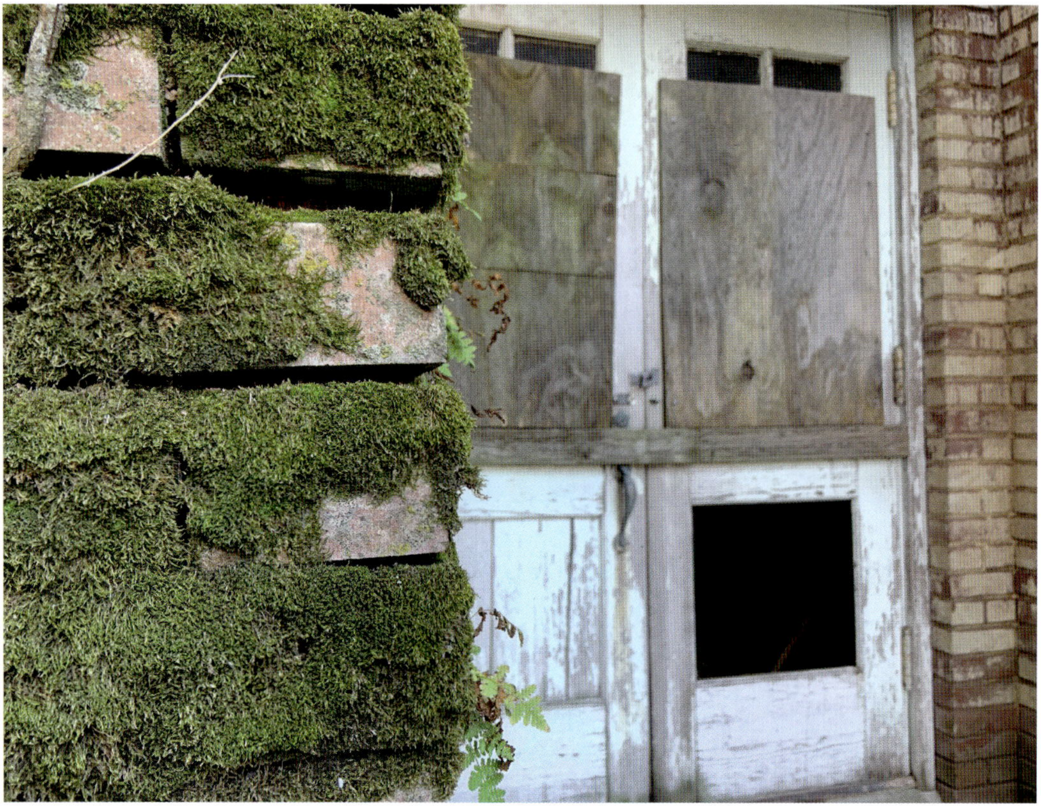

Moss covers some of the bricks at the side entrance at the abandoned school in Woodbine, November 2020.

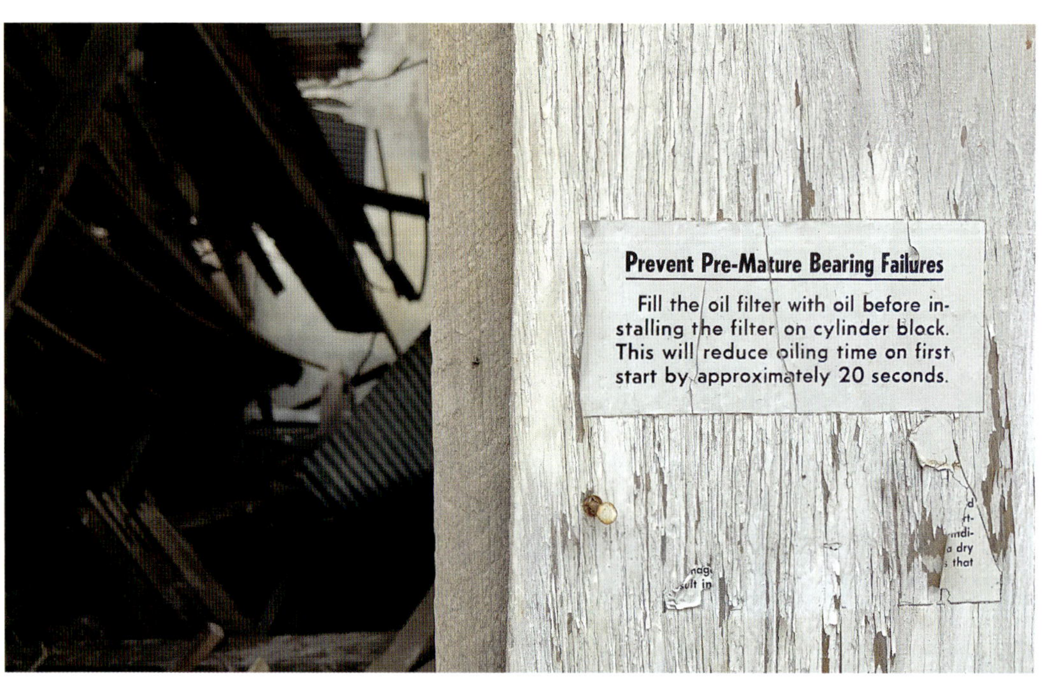

Safety instructions still on the wall of this collapsed garage in Elmo, November 2020.

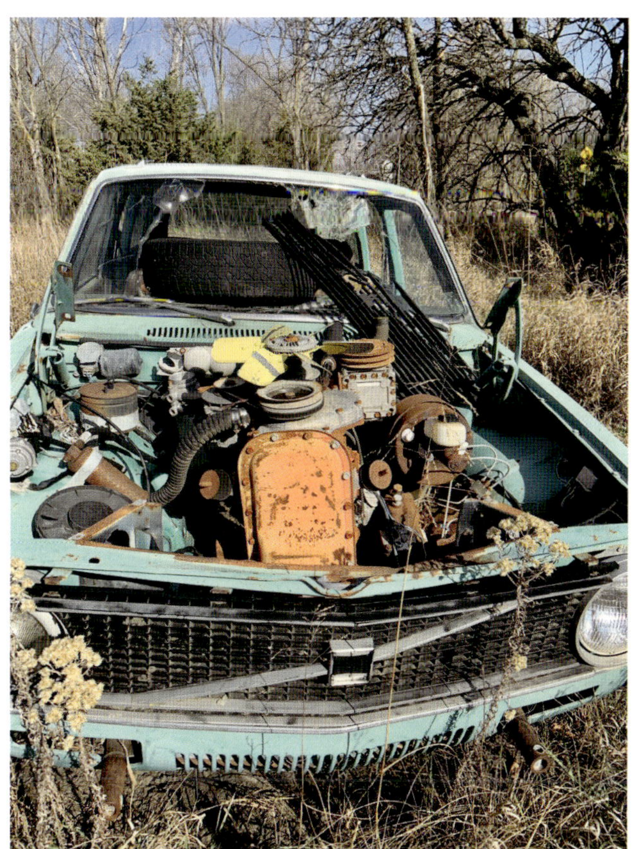

Right: An abandoned Volvo found in a field in Bushong, November 2020.

Below: Built in 1882, this church would later become a post office for the town of Skiddy, November 2020.

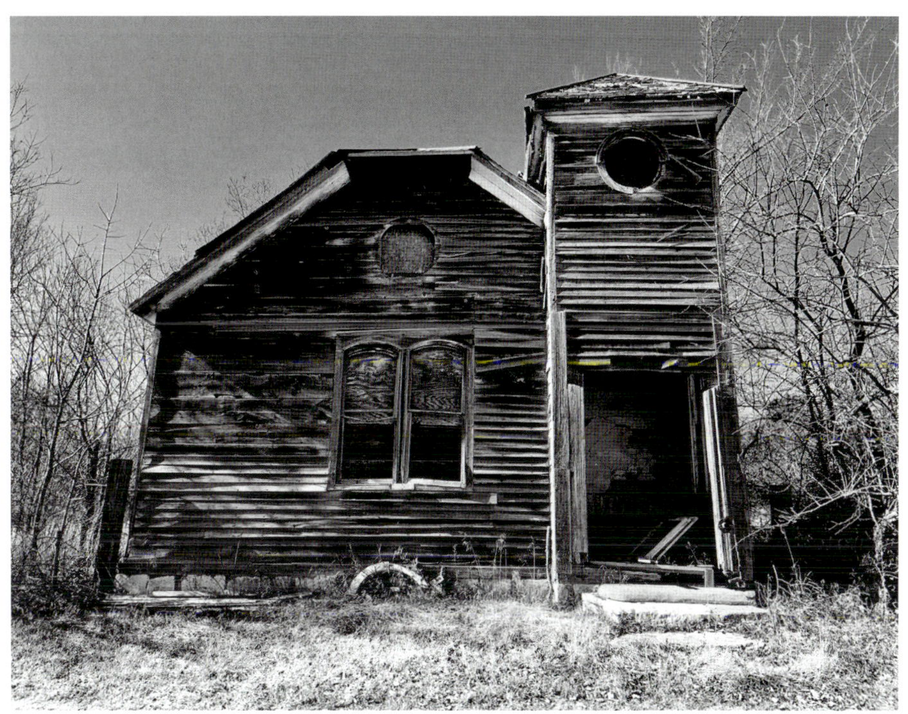

BIBLIOGRAPHY

Act of May 20, 1862 (Homestead Act), Public Law 37-64, 5/20/1862, Record Group 11; General Records of the United States Government; National Archives.

Boyer, W., "Personal Interview with Research Librarian," Lyon County History Center (January 2021).

Britannica, The Editors of Encyclopaedia, "Francisco Vazquez de Coronado," *Encyclopedia Britannica* (January 6, 2021; accessed April 3, 2021).

Brooks, R., "Bringing Back the Bushong Bank," *The Emporia Gazette* (September 25, 2018).

Center for Disease Control, "About Diphtheria," *National Center for Immunization and Respiratory Diseases* (May 26, 2020).

City of Cedar Point, "Drinkwater & Schriver Mill History" (2015)

Crowell, R., "Brief History of Allen County, Kansas: Mildred," *City of Iola, Allen County Kansas* (August 3, 2006).

Find A Grave, "Jackie Lee Davis," *Dunlap Colored Cemetery.* Memorial ID# 92556161 (June 25, 2012).

Find A Grave, "London A. Harness," *Dunlap Colored Cemetery.* Memorial ID# 34597262. (March 8, 2009).

Hagedorn, H., "Personal Interview with Historical Society Curator," Geary County Historical Society (January 2021).

"Has the New Town Been Named?" *The Kincaid Dispatch,* Vol. 20, No. 2 (August 2, 1907).

Hogan, S., "How Kansas City Became Home to the Nation's Official World War I Memorial," KCUR (November 9, 2018).

Johnson, B., "County Told to Bury Trash at Mildred," *The Iola Register,* Vol. 103, No. 67 (January 13, 2000).

Junction City Area Retired Teachers Association, "Project Heritage: History of Early Schools in Geary County Prior to Unification," Unified School District #475 of Geary County School Printer (1979).
Kansas Geological Survey, "Coronado Heights," *University of Kansas* (Accessed April 3, 2021).
Kansas Heritage Group. "Atchison, Topeka & Santa Fe Railroad," *Railroads in Kansas* (August 15, 2005).
Kansas Historical Society, "Coronado Heights," *National and State Registers of Historic Places* (Listed October 20, 2010).
Krieger, M.H., "Quivira," *Texas State Historical Association.*
League of Kansas Municipalities, "City of Elmdale," (July 10, 2019).
Luken, R., "Illegal Dump Gets Attention," *The Iola Register*, Vol. 103, No. 44 (December 15, 1999).
McDaniel, T., "*Our Land: A History of Lyon County Kansas*" (Emporia, Kansas: Emporia State Press, 1976).
McKenna, B., "Doc Bushong," *Society for American Baseball Research.*
McKenna, E., "Rural School Column," *The Iola Register* (May 2, 1940).
Minton, A., "Our History: The Spread of the One-Room School House," *The Morning Sun* (January 29, 2018).
North Lyon County Historical Society, "Bushong," *Town Histories* (2017).
"Poor Workman, The," *The Mildred Ledger*, Vol. 1, No. 52 (July 21, 1910).
Rogers, A., "Personal Interview with County Historian," Osage County Historical Society (January 2021).
United States Census Bureau, "Kansas: 2010 Population and Housing Unit Counts," *2010 Census of Population and Housing* (July 2012).
United States Census Bureau, "Kansas: 2019 Population and Housing Unit Counts," *2019 Census of Population and Housing* (May 24, 2020).
United State Dept. of the Interior National Park Service, "Cedar Point Mill," *National Register of Historic Places Registration Form* (December 20, 2006).
Weiser, K., "Neosho Falls, Kansas," *Legends of Kansas* (Updated July 2020).
Weiser-Alexander, K., "Dunlap, Kansas: A Freedman's Refuge," *Legends of Kansas* (Updated July 2020).
Weiser-Alexander, K., "Skiddy, Kansas: Railroad Ghost Town," *Legends of Kansas* (Updated September 2020).

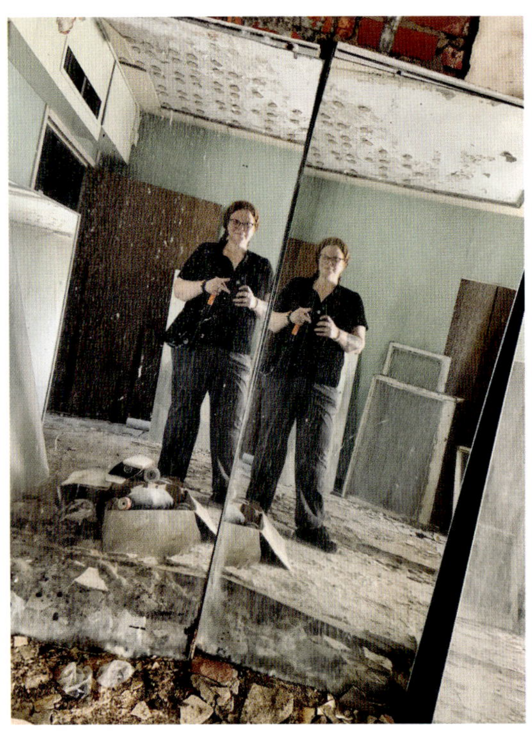

ABOUT THE AUTHOR

Regina Daniel specializes in urban exploration photography. She is also the owner and operator of Red Vixen Photography. Covering much of the Kansas City area and the surrounding vicinities, she has gone on to travel through six states in the Midwest doing her abandoned photography. What started as curiosity for the abandoned has turned into documenting the forgotten or lesser-known history lessons and photographing what has stood the test of time. That change from curiosity to preservation led her to write the *Abandoned Kansas City* book series and *Abandoned Picher, Oklahoma*. Regina's passion to photograph the abandoned will continue to have a driving force as long as progress continues to leave the old and obsolete behind for better and brighter tomorrows.